A WAY WITHOUT WORDS

A Guide
for
Spiritually Emerging Adults

Marsha Sinetar

PAULIST PRESS

NEW YORK/MAHWAH

Library of Congress Cataloging-in-Publication Data

Sinetar, Marsha.
    A way without words : a guide for spiritually emerging adults / by Marsha Sinetar.
      p.   cm.
    ISBN 0-8091-3303-2
    1. Spiritual life. 2. Spiritual exercises. 3. Diaries—Authorship—
Religious aspects—Christianity. 4. Bible. O.T. Psalms—Devotional use.
I. Title.
BV4501.2.S4728   1992
248.8'4—dc20   91-43891
                                               CIP

Published by Paulist Press
997 Macarthur Boulevard
Mahwah, New Jersey 07430

Printed and bound in the
United States of America

Also by Marsha Sinetar

Ordinary People as Monks and Mystics

Do What You Love, The Money Will Follow

Elegant Choices, Healing Choices

A Person Is Many Wonderful, Strange Things

Self-Esteem Is Just an Idea We Have About Ourselves

Living Happily Ever After

Developing a 21st Century Mind

Acknowledgements

I'm grateful that so many bright, talented people supported my efforts in this book. Pam Bacci handled all the word processing with her usual great skill, precision and speed, and Mary Tyner was a trustworthy researcher. Lyn DelliQuadri and Jill Hannum helpfully critiqued and edited this manuscript separately and at varying stages in its development. Kathleen (Trink) Morimitsu rescued the reading sessions with her educator's eye and expertise. Father Benedict Auer of St. Martin's College kindly reviewed my scriptural selections (even though I was a virtual stranger to him), and my, by-now, long-time Paulist Press friends showed enthusiasm for the book when it was done. My deepest thanks to all.

This book is dedicated to Mother Ann and Sister Mary Ruth, Monastery of the Visitation, Federal Way, Washington, with admiration and thanks.

God is love. Whoever lives in love,
lives in God,
and God in him.

1 John 4:16

TABLE OF CONTENTS

Part I

On Spirituality
as Higher Intelligence

How shall we sing the Lord's song
in a strange land?
Psalm 137:4

Divine love cannot
suffer to share with any
earthly love.

Catherine of Siena

INTRODUCTION

———————— ◊ ————————

The absence of language simply makes the presence of Silence more apparent.

Max Picard

A sophisticated priest, an effective communicator with worldly people, once went to a popular nightclub to tell the merry-makers about God. He wandered around the noisy club, amidst heavy smoke, drinkers, and loud music. He used street-language to say that God's way was friendly and sociable. Everyone was welcome. But those who heard him were basically honest and therefore skeptical. They unanimously rejected his message. To each other they said, "What kind of a religion is this whose agent's moral tone is so low that he courts us in such a common manner and arena? We'll stick to our own. At least there's no doubt what we are."

Following this story's wisdom, *A Way Without Words* encourages readers to explore their own spirituality privately and with dignity, in a personal journal. Or, if they seek out a discussion group, this book asks that they establish a proper, high-trust setting in which, with like-minded friends, they can elevate the topic. In matters of the spirit, it is best to raise, not lower, our values, language and expectations. However, by demystifying the subject of spirituality, by describing its practical benefits and everyday dimensions, I don't want to assume the watered-down or people-pleasing role of that priest. *A Way Without Words* is not for everyone.

◊

I originally intended this book simply as a study-guide for the readers of my first book, *Ordinary People as Monks and Mystics*. These are reflective adults who had asked for supplementary material. However, almost immediately I expanded the concept in order to include a loose structure and a contextual framework for individual use (or small group

3

discussions) which might interest readers who weren't familiar with that earlier book and who wanted to elevate their everyday values, align these with a truthful, spiritual way of being.

◊

There is healthy and growing interest in wholeness, what I and others call "self-actualization." Spirituality is an important aspect of this healthy, full personhood. Attending to our spiritual side is part of the continuing process of becoming a well-developed, integrated and mature human being.

Many equate religiousness and spirituality. To me, the two are related but unalike. Spirituality, as Chapter 1 elaborates, is a universal human quality. It is our inmost source, our essence or vitality—that which is elusive, mysterious, hidden and impossible to define in few sentences. But this does not mean that religion is useless; quite the opposite. Religion is that doctrine, or often fixed system of beliefs, through which we channel our finest spiritual energies. Religion lets us celebrate our spiritual life; through liturgy, hymns and sacred prayers we are empowered and renewed.

I realize that not all who want psychological health feel drawn toward either spiritual or religious matters. However, this book is for all those who actively want to integrate all their sub-selves and sides: cerebral, psycho-social, physical (or material) and spiritual. More than 80% of the 75 million baby boomers consider themselves religious and say they believe in an afterlife. Roughly 43 million people now attend church or synagogue services. But since many spiritual adults are disinclined to engage in formal religious worship, this book presents a reading and journal guide by which they may reevaluate that choice.

Millions of spiritually aware adults are either alienated from or disinterested in doctrinal, organized religions. Perhaps they are unsure or confused about their most sacred beliefs. They may feel slightly embarrassed about entertaining religious thoughts. Perhaps, like the opening story's nightclub goers, they feel a greater dignity in keeping their spirituality private. Maybe their views don't match those of their local church or temple. An articulate, thoughtful friend told me that he has a different understanding of God than is expressed through the world's scriptures. His sense is that "God" is a universal, cosmic intelligence, not a personal deity. This book examines the universality of spirituality and does so through familiar means.

◊

A Way Without Words employs many traditional religious terms: God's will, the kingdom of heaven, grace, faith and so on. Some readers will put this book aside simply because of its language.

Then there is the matter of God. St. Augustine's remark that God is closer to us than we are to ourselves, yet higher, sums up this word for me. I prefer the term "God" to such phrases as "higher self" or "higher power" probably because, to me, God manifests through and in us and in everything but is unlike anything that our mortal mind knows. These days I hear that many people now object to the words "God" and "Father" because these carry strong paternalistic or masculine biases. I don't feel this way and trust that in the silence of each session's meditations—which are, after all, deeply religious utterances of love—each reader can discover his or her own word for that divinity or sublime compassion which transforms us into perfect charity, whatever our backgrounds or linguistic preferences. Swami Vivekananda's comment on the word "God" is worth repeating. When asked, "Why do you use that old word, God?" he replied:

> Because it is the best word for our purpose; you cannot find a better word than that, because all the hopes, aspirations and happiness of humanity have been centered in that word. It is impossible now to change the word.
>
> ... Do you mean to say that because some fool says it is not all right, we should throw it away? ... Use the old word, only use it in the true spirit, cleanse it of superstition and realize fully what this great, ancient word means.[1]

◊

At first I questioned the usefulness of a book on adult spiritual growth. Who would seriously want to study such topics, either alone or in a group? How many readers would discipline themselves to take the time for such personal journal work or try to meet with others around the discussion/journal themes? Who would be open to an ecumenical text, much less one with such a diverse inclusion of interfaith passages? I was bound to offend somebody—if not everybody.

However, after deliberation, I'm convinced that contemporary adults do need and want a safe, responsible forum in which to explore their own spirituality—particularly if that forum (a journal or well-run group) furthers their self-understanding, their growth into full personhood and perhaps even their ability to empathically guide their children's spiritual development.

◊

Many people either ignore their religious and spiritual sensibilities or wonder where they can turn to discuss such topics. No one says how many adults, who believe either in a personal or a universal God, feel unsupported in their spirituality by their local minister, rabbi or priest. Therefore too many stay away from church or temple. One person told me that after several peak (or profound) spiritual experiences, her alienation from her church increased:

> Some of my greatest pain has come from realizing that others, my family and even my clergy, do not experience the same sense of knowing, or close contact with God, that I do. If I try to explain myself, I'm regarded as odd—as if I'm speaking a foreign language.

Apparently, people like this woman have not given up on God. They've just lost faith in organized religion. I hope some of these individuals will find their way to this book. They may use it to explore the difference between their religion and their spirituality, and to determine whether some formal religious practice might, in fact, enhance expression of their deepest, most sacred values. While this book is about the integrative process of spiritual emergence (i.e. coming into one's own, spiritually), it is not about religion, doctrine or denominational differences. Still *A Way Without Words* suggests that specific religious disciplines (particularly our devotion) help us become spiritually whole.

◊

Whatever our doctrinal heritage, almost all of us crave concrete ways to translate our delicate spiritual feelings into an integrated, truthful life. Later chapters explore the enormous practical benefits that stem from cultivating our spiritual depths. Our proper transformation of those finest, inner sensibilities into outer, daily functions empowers us, makes us capable and effective. Compassion, honesty, responsible right action, self-discipline and integrity are spiritual qualities; these bring personal power and supernatural purpose to our life, draw us into our own light.

◊

It is not my aim to convince anyone that God exists. Part I simply attempts to show that spirituality is an intelligence in its own right, one that adds luster, meaning and consequential depth or mystery to our lives, just as does analytical or musical ability.

I have selected scriptural passages (the Psalms mostly), lines of poetry, journal and discussion topics to draw out and cultivate readers' affection or friendliness toward others (and ourselves), and to regenerate awe, wonder and reverential devotedness to God. *A Way Without Words* is an ecumenical overview of spiritual emergence in adulthood. The book's title refers to its worshipful reading process (presented in Part II). This strives to entrain interior silence, love of liturgy and respect for the world's sacred writings into readers' awareness.

The sessions (of Part II's chapters) introduce a reflective reading process that can be practiced by anyone. Each session entertains a theme for the corresponding reading, journal writing or dialogue. For those who want to extend the session's process to group discussions, an *appendix for study-circles* is included at the end of this book. It suggests some ways in which readers, facilitators and group members may use this book. The journal questions and follow-up considerations are designed to clarify a current dilemma or reveal our way of responding to it.

◊

Even though I've written this book from my own Christian perspective, many who find value here will fall outside this framework. This book is open and friendly to doctrinal and philosophical diversity. Part II's core of the Psalms as a liturgical motif tries to make *A Way Without Words* easily modifiable to the numerous paths that spiritual seekers take. For instance, some readers may skip over the Psalms (or the other, optional biblical passages) in order to spend time with their favorite poems or what I've termed interfaith passages. Others will relish the Psalms and some may even be drawn into regular Bible reading sessions as a result of reacquainting themselves with the Psalms. Still others may prefer to find (or write) their own favored poems, myths or diary entries to replace or augment the silent readings. All this (like all specific religious sensibility and commitment) is, of course, up to each individual's conscious, adult choice.

◊

However else we choose to think of these religious themes, to me God is Love. Most important is that love (in its broadest, impersonal and compassionate sense) may increase in whoever reads and works with this material. Whoever we are, any addition of love invariably encourages, integrates and enlivens us. Of course, love has countless forms and faces. It transcends physical passion or exclusivity. It moves beyond the personal into universal spheres. It stirs improved self-attitudes (including tolerance for our own flaws and our struggle to express ourselves or be authentic). Love stimulates all healing—it doesn't just build high regard for self-and-others but also seeds actual bodily improvements. Love extends our ability to make active, bold or risky choices. It renews our resourceful, creative drives. All these benefits, and more, demonstrate that wholesome love heals, guides and improves life.

◊

Part I reviews the problem we in western culture face in terms of our relative spiritual impoverishment of language, support systems and even practical encouragement. For those who find themselves maturing into psychologically whole, full persons, there are few avenues in which to discuss this transformation. This transformation, not religious doctrine, is my context for this book. I only skirt the topic. Part II and an Appendix describe the reading process I call A Way Without Words. Its structure, the purpose of silence, the group sessions as a whole, and the role that regular, meditative reading might play in our overall development forms the center of Part II. This introduces the reading sessions themselves. These sessions are modules to be utilized by individual readers who want to work alone (say in a journal) or to be expanded to discussion-group use (by facilitators who work with groups). Or, the sessions can be used for both journal and discussion (or study-circle) exploration.

Whether we study on our own or with others, the crux of our work is discovering the images, conscious acts, language and ideals for our own spirituality and then expressing these in everyday life. Ultimately, what we think, say and do is our religion.

◊

Ecumenical and Inter-Faith Elements

I felt an urgency to write a book (and create a discussion-context) that reinforces the traditional western worldview *and* transmits respect for the age-old universal ideas about spiritual emergence. These ideas are also present in the rich heritage of eastern philosophies and religious literature. To grow secure in our specific religious loyalties, narrower doctrinal texts and spiritual formation programs are certainly warranted. Our devotion and subsequent identification is more intense and focused when we are single-minded. However, in terms of the psycho-social issues of spiritual emergence generally—the human side of this transformation—a wider framework seems more appropriate. The big-picture shows us the unifying, and transcultural, stages and elements of our shared human experience. We gain sympathetic appreciation of other seekers the world over.

That venerable metaphysical philosopher Dr. Paul Brunton suggested that Christians might interpret and understand their own religion more completely if they empathically studied other, eastern religions, especially the Indian ones.[2] I would only add: vice versa.

Above and beyond simply appreciating our own religious heritage, we become most fully self-realized when we comprehend the potential (and even the pain or momentary discords) inherent in spiritual maturity. Usually, such maturity evidences itself as we sense kinship between ourselves and others—no matter how different they are doctrinally.

A scientist I met on a plane told me he was always touched by the basic human dignity of people he met when traveling around the world. "I'm not a religious man, but this commonality links me with others in an almost mystical way."

This transcultural affection can be cultivated within the context of our own life, whatever our worldview or personal creed. Doing so helps develop our spiritual wholeness and even increases our commitment to a formal religious life. This happens because love—transcultural affection—understanding of others, cooperation, empathy and expanded, deepened loyalties are all signs that spirituality's special love, *agape,* is alive in us. With spiritual maturity, we are enhanced as disciples of any creed.

The Hindu proverb, "To those in whom Love dwells the whole world is one family," expresses this universal, spiritual appreciation (or *agape*) exactly; this quality is positively transforming, deeply regenerating to the one possessing it.

I state throughout that *agape* is impersonal. Not exactly an emotion, *agape* still warmly alters our feeling-life. Perhaps it is a "meta-emotion"—an overarching quality that gives us strength to go against our baser feelings or purposefully counter the wishes of important people in order to do God's will. *A Way Without Words* examines many facets of this impersonal, "irregular" love.

◊

A Way Without Words invites reflective adults into truthful dialogue with themselves or with like-minded friends in a wide-open, global setting. Truth like this—as is expressed in the Psalms or other sacred texts quoted—is simply love. Such truth is appreciated by all who receive it with a large mind and a generous, open-heart.

This reading process provides a context for diversely oriented readers to explore their own and others' spirituality—not simply to learn more about the specific doctrines or rules of their faith. First, we realize that we, as spiritually minded people, long for God, for inner peace and love. Next, we consciously choose the means or specific commitments by which we believe we can best unite ourselves with his will and Love.

◊

Our yearning to know God, to be known by him; our desire to be good, decent persons and to relate to others on some high plane of simple, easy cooperation; our childlike, innocently motivated wish to express love in our daily life (e.g. through work, choices and relationships)—all these point to a supernatural impulse. These drives are prompted by human spirituality, and every emotionally healthy person feels some of these impulses from time to time.

Both the content and the process of *A Way Without Words* are designed to stimulate inter-faith, ecumenical and personal exploration. The journal exercises and discussion themes help readers examine the way their ordinary choices, commitments and relinquishments build—or defeat—spiritual wholeness. Couples (or families) can also use this reading process. It is exciting to think that some readers, as yet unfamiliar with the scope of sacred literature, will be so touched by the psalmists that they will delve more deeply into the Psalms—on their own (or continue to read other scriptures) after finishing this book. Some readers may introduce their children to these devotional poems and celebrations of God, and this too can initiate a memorable family tradition.

◊

A *Way Without Words* is not a theological or doctrinal text. It does highlight some of the subjective, practical sides of adult spirituality. Readers may find it necessary to "protect" their doctrinal beliefs, while reflecting on—and expanding—their own spiritual universe. It is entirely possible to hold different ideas in our mind at the same time; mature thinkers do this routinely.

It is also important to support the spiritual life of others while discussing these topics. By this I mean we read in a way that honors what we believe even while listening to others, honoring their feelings, their subjective, spiritual life and their worldview.

The ancient Christian thinker Origen wrote that when we draw into our own concept of God notions that are out of place there, we "take the name of the Lord God in vain." But he also advised us to verbalize our inner sentiments in a way that "helps the souls [of others] bear fruit."[3] This dual assignment seems well within the capabilities of emotionally secure adults and serves as a practical, kind ground rule for our readings or talks with others about these issues.

◊

Just as there are discernible patterns and values in individual spiritual growth, so there are patterns—repeating spiritual motifs—in essentially all major religions—for instance, individual faith in a higher being (or supernatural force or forces) and strict, clear behavioral precepts to guide believers toward "the good." These global rules and taboos differ in their forms and doctrines, of course, but the undergirding, eternal themes do not.

As we study these issues (especially as we realize that many of these are held universally sacred) we may discover that religion—the specific articles or dogma of our own creed or faith—can help us approach our God, not hinder us. Religion can encourage us, as believers, toward an effective, loving and faith-filled way of life. Both universal spiritual impulses and specific religious worship deepen human spirituality.

◊

In suggesting that the content be ecumenical, I refer to the idea of establishing greater cooperation and mutual respect among all peoples—not just between Christians and Jews but also among Christians of different denominations and among them and everyone else. I employ the word ecumenical to mean that large-minded generous-heartedness through which we each discover what issues of faith unite us to fellow humans around the planet. As we build transcultural affection, learning to appreciate our commonality with others, we can establish a more humane and fully human world. This appreciation happens consciously, over time, as each one reaches out to others on a small scale and in a personal way.

◊

This book repeats a personal bias: It is possible to have the soul of a monk or a mystic without being religiously cloistered. Being a "monk" and a "mystic" is a state of mind and heart—an inner posture. This elevated, perhaps primitive, way of being is available to all people regardless of age, gender, culture, religion, education, or socio-economic background. This consecrated inner stance is one of consciousness, not simply one of outer form. Spiritual wholeness—holiness—is not reserved for those who are in some way "odd," formally ordained or intellectually elite. Spiritual completeness is gained by anyone who grows into closer union with God and who then expresses—that is, lives—his or her holy union in some productive and loving way, say in service to society or as a good parent or as a gifted artist or as an ethical business person. I hope that this book encourages such union, the benchmark of which is love. Only through love can our personal development be fully and uniquely merged with the long-term best interests of our community.

◊

"In the beginning was the Word, and the Word was with God, and the Word was God." A Way Without Words means to get us back to silent beginnings, emptiness and to our own authentic life—to the audible interior word of our souls that shapes and forms us into love.

◊

Perhaps the chief business of life is simply to learn how to love. The nineteenth century saint, Thérèse of Lisieux, who died at age 24, summed up this primordial assignment of existence: ". . . It's love! To love, to be loved, and to return to the earth to make love loved . . ."

◊ ◊

1. OUR SPIRITUAL INTELLIGENCE

◊

All beings exist in me. Remember that.
Bhagavad-Gita
Chapter 9

The word *spiritual* implies any number of diverse drives to enrich and express our inner life. Spirituality stimulates our healings (psychological or physical) while stirring our feelings of greater affection, friendliness or cooperation (for ourselves and others). Indeed *any* infusion of love or inspiration to our thought, feeling or action—any movement of will toward kindness, patience and charity—indicates the presence of spirituality. These are what scripture commonly terms the "fruits of the spirit."

As we raise our spiritual intelligence, we progressively learn new abilities that enable us to live in love. This understanding (contrary to what some might think) is incredibly practical in real-life terms. However, a high spiritual I.Q. can be disruptive. Our wisdom, intuition and sensibilities may take us away from the world. This chapter examines some of the more unsettling aspects of this higher human intelligence.

Religion vs. Spirituality

Religion is our particular, potentially fixed, system of beliefs. This includes all the special rites, language and observances defining our chosen practice of devotion. Religion is also more: it is our worldview, our way of revering specific people, values, politics or philosophies. It is creed—encompassing not just God or our thoughts about the supernatural, but life itself. (For a robust discussion of this, see M. Scott Peck, *The Road Less Traveled.*)

We often speak about people's work being their religion, or we talk of their devotion to money, family, spouse, or child. Religion is how we structure or encase our beliefs. It can be defined, packaged, boxed up,

15

discussed, dissected. To me, even atheists seem religious. They believe in something: life's finiteness, their own mortality, death's finality or certain humanistic principles.

Spirituality, on the other hand, is soft, unfixed, untidy, and potentially embarrassing. It isn't easy to talk about the experiences of our own spirit. After all, where and what is "spirit"? That which undergirds our conscious life (the vital principle in us) is elusive, hidden and mysterious.[1] Spirituality is our tendency toward the ineffable core of our creative self. It is a mystical sense, the subtle perception and feeling of sacredness that drives our quest for God, overarching meaning or purpose. It is our love for family or that which gives us a big, life vision.

When we discuss someone's spirit, we mean that person's "essence or animating elements that pervade and temper thought, feeling or emotion."[2] Thinking of our spirituality, we consider all those delicate, most tender variables of our own nature—our own ineffable animating essence, that unseen energy, awareness or source which lives in us, which "pervades and tempers" our thought, feelings and actions. Many people find agreement about their particular, fixed belief-systems by calling themselves Buddhists, Christians, Hindus or Jews. But no two people, even within a given religion, have identical spirits. Human language cannot precisely define or articulate our spiritual experience. One person, hearing that this book was called *A Way Without Words*, asked, "How can you even write about spirituality when it can't be languaged?" Walt Whitman said,

> When I undertake to tell the best, I find I cannot.
> My tongue is ineffectual on its pivots,
> My breath will not be obedient to its organs,
> I become a dumb man.[3]

Unchurched and non-religious people also have a spiritual life. Everyone is spiritual to one degree or another, although many people don't admit it and find it uncomfortable or inappropriate to discuss.

While spirituality helps us merge our inner experience with that of others, religion can separate. The universality of spirit is explained in the Bhagavad-Gita's line, "I am in every religion as a thread through a string of pearls."

When we think, "I'd love to get to know Mary (or John) better," we may mean that we want to understand that person's spirit. We seek information about whatever animates and brings that person to life.

Our spirituality enlivens our relationships. I've heard men say that women are most attractive when they're enthusiastic. Said one bachelor, "Show me a woman who's in love with something outside herself—anything, her home, family, kids, work—and I'm turned on. I love to see a woman's face light up when she's talking about her interests." He was expressing the way his own spirit "lights up" (i.e. is turned on) when a woman's spirit is well lit. Her light switches on his own animating essence.

People's spiritual life is linked to whatever fascinates, interests or engages them. Perhaps this is one underlying meaning of that cryptic biblical precept, "The joy of the Lord is my strength." When we touch our deepest fulfillments or gifts and the wonderment of our own unseen energies, we are instantly invigorated. These fulfillments unite us not only with our physical or sensory natures but also with our subtlest inner values and tones of consciousness. The deeper we go into these interior essences, the more strength, health, vitality and "is-ness" we absorb.

My doctor recently described the birth of his first child, expressing distinctly spiritual, not religious, sentiments:

> The first time I looked into my son's eyes, I saw right down into the core of his little being. And he looked into mine. I felt we'd known each other before. I've never had that feeling, the sense that he and I are one, completely united, part and parcel of one integral experience.

As later pages describe, *religion* may be an inspired gift. It allows us to activate and express our thanks, our devotion, our single-mindedness. Religion channels our identity to God, joins us with him, unites our mind's images with his mystery. This point is relevant for all who hope to increase their spiritual I.Q. To me, the saints of all religions are spiritual giants: Whatever their doctrinal path, they possess inordinate "natural" gifts and high native aptitude for supernatural relationship. Through our religious images, precepts, heroes and heroines, our conscious mind is encoded with the attitudes, behaviors and values our spirituality craves. While it is each one's responsibility to consciously choose his or her religion (and thereby control personal spiritual development), spirituality per se is universal—like creativity, rationality, a sense of humor, pathos or joy, it is a particularly human facet of intelligence. To one degree or another, we all possess it.

Spiritual Intelligence

> The wisdom of the world is foolishness before God.
>
> 1 Cor 3:19

Whenever we feel loving union with someone or something beyond ourselves, our spiritual intelligence is influencing us. Loving union has, of course, various levels of maturity. One aim of this book is to help ourselves elevate our level of love so that we are brighter in the way we express it. For some, self-love is the extent to which they are capable of feeling love. Self-loving parents love their children exploitively, from a frame of reference of what a child can or cannot do for them. Self-loving spouses love their mates in the same way. To self-loving people, love is something one *feels* but not necessarily something one is or does. For others, physical "love" or romantic love is as far as this affection goes. By contrast, the sense of union experienced by spiritually maturing individuals suggests responsible action: "He and I are completely united, part and parcel of one integral experience. Therefore, as I treat the other, I treat myself." Those who feel this way take responsible action for their own young, and for all children and people around the globe.

Our simplest choices reveal the level, presence or degree of our spiritual intelligence. Probably everyone has had an intuition that says, "I'll do this, as the spirit moves me." The inclination to listen to some inner impulses marks spiritual intelligence at work. The more this mind guides our way of being, the more spiritually whole we can become. This doesn't mean we abandon logical or rational thinking but rather that we intuit when to use which intelligence.[4]

A friend described a recent, major career move. He gave spiritual reasons for his transition:

> When I was about 4 or 5 I had an adventurer in me. I'd go on
> all those backwoods and camping trips. My mind traveled into
> distant, unknown places, even outer space.

Somewhere along the line, I lost that boy, rejected that exploring part of myself. Well, last year, at the ripe old age of forty, that little boy returned. One bright Saturday morning, I woke up with an urge to go hiking. I was excited, charged-up—emotions I'd forgotten. So, I put on my backpack and left.

Thirty-four miles later I knew what I wanted to do with the rest of my life: Live it. I finally understood the scriptural edict: "If you try to save your life, you'll lose it . . ." Shortly after that, with some plotting and planning, I quit my job. Now I'm freelancing. More to the point, I'm alive again—and so thankful for it.

Through an emotional impulse, and a mix of logical and "illogical" thinking, my friend consciously chose to move on. Much of his knowing about what to do next came from a wordless state. Part II describes an ongoing reading process of self-inquiry themes and questions. These can encourage our own wordless knowing. Silence, the pure objective awareness of being, is our "way without words." It opens us up to our deepest spiritual awareness. Silence is fertile soil. What we receive from this rich ground depends on what we put into it: our attention, our images and ideas or the words we ingest from what we hear or from reading material, and, yes, even our specific religious, worshipful devotion are all seeds that we ourselves plant in our inmost silence. People who remain unconscious about their own spiritual and religious life seem much like irresponsible farmers: They devalue the land entrusted to their care.

Behavioral "Fruits" of Higher Intelligence

Excluding instantaneous conversions, only as we consciously serve our "inner person's" directives do we grow whole. To paraphrase Carl Jung, self-realized persons ascend to wholeness consciously. They consciously separate themselves from mindless, consensus thinking; they consciously devote themselves to the demands of their vocation (i.e. to the realities of full, authentic personhood); consciously they translate "into their own individual reality what leads to ruin if lived unconsciously."[5]

Listening to our inner voice does not mean we are neurotic or in any way anti-social. In this book as in my others, I write about *optimal* adult functioning and describe how self-actualizing adults use their interior drives to contribute to others. This means turning spiritual energies into fulfilling interpersonal relationships or employing these simply to grow able to love and work productively. Compassion, creativity and humane, humanitarian love are all spiritual qualities. These develop as we do—as our interior sensitivities emerge. Mature spirituality means discerning Ultimate Reality—not living in unreality.

There *is* a difference between being an anti-social, neurotic misfit and being a saint, although each of these roles means we attend to interior realities and may appear unusual, quirky or highly idiosyncratic. Scripture teaches us that "by their fruits ye shall know them." The spiritually mature increasingly devote their lives to the lavish, bright insights of pure objectivity. They do so in order to know and demonstrate God—not to glorify themselves, gain personal (i.e. worldly) power or exploit others by some sort of crude one-upmanship.

We might identify with this contributive, compassionate frame of mind yet not know exactly how, or why, we are changing. Sometimes people feel restless—not themselves. One person said she was excited (and scared) about her future prospects. She felt an early inkling of inner direction (and was charmed by her interior world) but couldn't tell where she was headed:

> As yet, I don't fit that advanced, highly reflective profile of many people whom I sense to be deeply spiritual. I'm active— a real participator. I use my energy and capabilities to initiate and implement large, complex ventures. I'm also involved in my community—church, social and even fund-raising. However, I sense I'm changing.

> Lately, I've given up most of my volunteer positions, live a less busy, less "worldly" life. I read more, limit the number of hours I watch T.V., and turn off radios. (Previously I had music blaring all the time.) I'm moving toward my own inner core. Several years ago, I wouldn't have known what that phrase meant. Now, I want to move—that is, grow—quickly.

For the ordinary person, behavioral benchmarks exist for self-evaluation along this path. If we simply review a few of the predictable characteristics that spiritually healthy people share, we can tell if we are developing the positive side of our emerging self. In varying degrees, the spiritually healthy move into unitive consciousness.[6] This mind enhances their life and generates compassion and feelings of aliveness. The spiritually mature have many traits in common, among which are:

◊ They have a highly developed sense of ethics, aesthetics or universal order.

◊ They experience their work (and/or daily activity) as devotional, as calling or as service.

◊ They design their life to be as simple, orderly and uncomplicated as possible, and/or single-mindedly devote themselves to discernible, life-affirming values, relationships and principles (Professor Warren Bennis' comment on leaders, "They're all of a piece," fits the spiritually healthy as well).

◊ They possess a superior, objective grasp of reality (e.g. solve problems ingeniously; function productively in diverse, real-world or interpersonal context *because* their perceptual context is coherent and whole, not fragmented).

◊ They demonstrate connectedness, sense themselves part of a living, interactive cosmos.

◊ They are good-humored, sometimes childlike, and (paradoxically) healthfully skeptical.

◊ They are both personally and socially responsible, willing to consider, forecast and accept the consequences of their actions. They exhibit active, natural self-control, rather than requiring externally imposed controls. (Maslow's thought applies: it is only to self-actualizing people that we can say, "Do what you will, it will probably turn out all right."[7])

◊ They love and work productively. (Here, Erich Fromm's precept is valid: "Love [is] dependent on the absence of narcissism, it requires the development of humility, objectivity and reason. One's whole life must be devoted to this aim."[8])

Spirituality's Practical Benefits and Demands

Saints, legendary artists, poets, composers, inventors and spiritual leaders illustrate the gains that society accrues when people develop their spiritual life—their inmost animating energies, drives and awarenesses. Even a random listing of names of contemporary greats illustrates how richly diverse these animating energies can be:

Bruno Bettelheim, Aaron Copeland, Jacques Cousteau, e.e. cummings, Dorothy Day, Feodor Dostoevski, Mary Baker Eddy, Albert Einstein, Mahatma Gandhi, Buckminster Fuller, Kahlil Gibran, Ortega y Gasset, Billy Graham, Dag Hammarskjöld, Ernest Holmes, Hermann Hesse, Helen Keller, Nelson Mandela, Martin Luther King, Jr., Thomas Merton, John Muir, Cardinal Newman, Mother Teresa, Masaharu Taniguichi, Bishop Desmond Tutu, Miguel Unamuno and innumerable others have left us a rich spiritual legacy from their well-developed inner vision and their other gifts.

So it is with us. Whether we believe in destiny, God or our inner, higher power, as we nurture and productively express our talents, fascinations and inner realities, we bring fresh ideas and our own, enhanced presence into being. Actualizing these higher capacities—our need and drive to go beyond ourselves—we serve progress. This is so, no matter how seemingly insignificant our abilities.

Spirituality is not just an abstract, blissed-out or purposeless emotion, nor is spiritual development an out-of-reach, mythical goal. Spirituality is an intelligence in its own right: useful, tactical and immensely creative. With a high spiritual I.Q. we gain insight, wisdom, visionary or strategic, big-picture perceptual skills and the knack of right action. Our spiritual depths house our life's most positive force. This has everything to do with our growing in personal power and tangible, lasting, real-world effectiveness and little to do with that dreamy, aimless quality so often equated (in the popular culture's mind) with spirituality. If aimlessness exists in one with spiritual drives, it is either temporary or caused by other factors.

To increase spiritual intelligence and behave in a productive way we first give of ourselves. For example, we will properly direct our attention or improve our self-discipline and our responsibility-taking skills. This means our finest inner directives ask us to slowly turn down the sound system of the world. These choices teach us the everlasting law: first we give, then we get. Over time, practically anyone who consciously wills it can develop his or her awareness, talent and full humanity. This affords concrete benefits, not the least of which is that life (given its revised, wholesome perspective) gets organized around the values and behaviors that serve both self and other. Included in this constellation of benefits are a host of improved personal skills . . .

◊ We begin to gain "whole-sight," non-dualistic perception.

◊ Our intuition is enhanced; we are guided from within ourselves, supernaturally.

◊ Our interpersonal life becomes more refined, less problematic.

◊ We revere life, order, and our own unique experience.

Not a few growing pains are stirred by such improvements. As spiritually emerging adults, one problem that we face is isolation—the sense that no one else understands our experience. In part, this is accurate. When, for instance, we lose our appetite for the world's tidbits of pleasure, it is hard to find words to explain this to others (perhaps even those dear to us) who are still hungry for the old fulfillments. Later chapters, and Part II's readings, explore the issues of isolation and other concerns of those who travel a spiritual path. Those reborn into God realize their earthly realm as alien. With the psalmist they wonder, "How shall we sing the Lord's song in a strange land?"

Interpersonal Refinements

Without question, mature spirituality refines and purifies our interpersonal life, usually by degrees. We take three steps forward into a healthier interactive style and two steps back (or even four). Confusion, guilt or shame abounds if we're not vigilant. Surely this is where inner principalities war.

Consider the person who, after years of self-betrayal, doubt and fear, "suddenly" refuses to be victimized by others. Clearly the seeds of spirituality have grown enough for good to finally triumph over evil. I have known those who, in much this way, abruptly become sensitive to crude, unwholesome (i.e. sinful, evil, hypocritical) behaviors and who only then change their life for the better.

Many people report spontaneously leaving psychically suffocating friends, relatives and colleagues. An exceptional friend, a devout, twenty-year meditator, says she can no longer watch movies or TV shows when meanness, violence or pornography are dramatized. In early childhood I intuitively recoiled from unstable, excessively possessive relatives and negotiated a way to leave the family nest before my fourteenth birthday. Years later I read the histories of exemplary individuals who, as children, also fled their homes. Some left prior to the age of ten. These spiritually precocious youngsters left in order to be free of the enslaving, over-emotional "love" that prohibits development of spiritual autonomy.[9] In just this way, many adults can feel a need to pull away from unwhole-some, restrictive affection in order to grow. Our emerging spirituality generates pain and loss by making us *want* to relinquish some of our comforts.

In the interest of self-realization, we yearn to be rid of all that belongs to our false self, our "old" person. Perhaps we press toward some hard-to-name goal that stretches us beyond our present comfort-zone. We may adopt healthier, more moderate personal habits.

The person who was addicted to work, status or making money may instead spend time alone or with loved ones. Someone else, who has been understimulated, may crave excitement in the form of travel or ca-reer advancement. Unhappily married people may summon the courage to seek counseling where they will face the unattractive—often unac-ceptable—side of their relationship (and themselves). Or, accepting the inevitable, they find the consequence of separation or divorce both physically and psychically painful.

A friend of mine started meditating. He had never intended to give up smoking. Suddenly he found the taste and smell of tobacco offensive. Still, it took him two more years to give up cigarettes. This physical ex-ample shows us how much work there is to do in bringing our behavior into line with our new standards, values and self-expectations.

A woman I met while conducting a workshop had been sexually abused by her father. When the seminar turned to the topic of forgive-ness, she left the room. Later, in the hall, I saw that she'd been crying. She said that forgiving her father, not just with words, but with true, heart-felt reconciliation, was her as-yet unrealized goal. She said she didn't know how to live without rage.

It's one thing to say you forgive someone, and quite another to so thoroughly assimilate and be done with anger that we get on with our life, and let go of the past.

Somehow she knew that, even though she didn't have to visit her abuser, forgiveness meant completing (i.e. finishing and then assimilating) the memory fully. When we truly forgive others, all that's left of anger is thankfulness for being alive. We then forget our abusers, wish them well and do "get on with" our lives.

Spiritual advancement introduces loss, as the examples above show. Inner shifts prompt outer revisions. This is what spiritual growth is all about. Later sessions explore the various practical aspects of such shifts.

As we grow older, spiritual emergence dictates its own special urgency. People for whom the first part of life has been unsatisfying now make a determined effort to change the second half. Their moves are fueled by their reverence for life and by the growing sense that they have limited time to honor their talents and gifts. Despite fear, they surrender themselves to the call and law of their own being. This was so for a financial executive who rerouted himself to graduate school for an advanced degree in science:

> [Before experiencing certain inner growth] I felt science was (for me) just a diversion. Now I see that idea itself was resistance—a way of thwarting my best self. I kept my talents away from myself by a belief in the silliness of something I loved.

> How things will develop I don't know. I'm assailed by fear at this point and have real sadness for the friends I'm leaving. I'm at a point of no return in this transition—there's no way to go but onward.

Spiritual and emotional maturity coincide. Former UN Secretary General Dag Hammarskjöld (now deceased) commented that maturity is a time when we stop hiding our strengths from ourselves out of fear and begin to live at our best level—instead of below it.

The Redirection of Attention

These internal shifts frequently follow a predictable route: As the material, everyday world fades into the background of our awareness, spiritual concerns take center stage. We start to examine not outer but inner realities and live by the rule "Be in the world but not of it." To accommodate this redirection of attention, we revise both inconsequential and significant habits. We may alter daily routines, structure our time differently or perhaps change the way we work.

For instance, people once motivated by purely competitive career considerations often find themselves eager for an authentic, meaningful vocation: an intrinsic calling, necessitating both a personal and a professional coming-of-age. A friend told me about a well-paid executive who decided to take early retirement to open a pub. This had been his dream since visiting England. Others find that they have much inner repair work to do before they can reach their goals. For them, therapy or group counseling precedes new achievements. Their movement toward growth is rarely easy or instant.

Each altered course or shift in worldview also requires us to relinquish what has been. Before gaining something new, we release former things. This development, when it occurs in the collective consciousness, upsets the status quo of community, institutions and family habits. The best example of this was the peace movement during the 1960s, when the traditional views of young and old alike were shaken by a mass movement of revised values. In the life of the individual, a similar clash and an experiential anarchy seems the norm: this means we don't know which end is up.

Heightened Spiritual Intelligence Disrupts Normal Life

Disorder or confusion arrives whenever we revise our inner and outer life. How we deal with these alterations depends on our way of handling problems and our own psychological history. For instance, some tidy and methodical people try, as best they can, to plan for all of life's upheavals. Their taxes, insurance policies and closets are neat and orderly. Sometimes these meticulous types suffer more during spiritual upheavals than do spontaneous, easy-going ones.

But few of us are prepared for the momentous disruption that interior shifts can bring. Reading about other people's experience is never like living through our own. Spiritual emergence stimulates a fairly reliable emotional pattern which is described in one way or another in all the world's sacred literature, myths and folklore. The moth headed into a flame is an apt and frequent spiritual metaphor: there is self-immolation inherent in our transpersonal search. Conversions of habits, values and relationships amount to a series of small deaths which we ourselves set up. Like moths, we are drawn to these dissolutions.

As we give ourselves over to new loyalties and affections, those to whom we might turn for consolation may misinterpret and misunderstand us. We forget that friends, colleagues and therapists are simply ordinary people with fixed belief-systems of their own. Counselors, as one example, are by no means "enlightened" as a group; few (save the best of the best) are even gifted enough to have developed what has been called a "private science." Most obediently follow their textbooks, teachers and mentors.

The psychoanalytic tradition has historically discounted the mystical dimension of life and the reality behind it. If we have had peak experiences (i.e. out-of-time or spaceless moments of rapture and ecstatic insight) or if our spirituality includes mystical or inexplicable elements, there is no reason to expect that our self-disclosures will meet with much empathy. As a matter of fact, with the exception of Jung (who seemed himself a mystic) the major schools of traditional psychoanalysis have defined mystics as hysterics or worse.

Even organized religion (and thus spiritual directors or ministerial counselors) may be unfriendly to the mystical perspective since it is always an individual phenomenon, hard to describe, and generally subversive to institutional processes and objectives. Superior, unconventional thinkers, psychiatrists like, say, Dr. Thomas Szasz or Dr. R.D. Laing, have written of the power struggle that ensues when religious or spiritual people walk through the doors of insensitive, controlling counselors expecting to be understood. We should enter at our own risk, realizing that the average psychoanalyst is fluent in the language and cognitive constructs of pathology, neurosis and "the known," while the spiritually emerging (especially the mystics in the bunch) speak of things supernatural and the unknown. This is not your marriage made in heaven.

For instance, the buzz-phrase "middle age crisis" is an easy one to affix to those who leave posh jobs for simple, low paying ones. Other behaviors can also be called foolhardy, indulgent or even irresponsible. A woman friend just sold her business to work at little pay for Habitat. One friend leaves his prospering business every other month to visit an ashram (cloistered spiritual setting or retreat) in India. He studies with, and receives spiritual direction from, his Master, a noted guru. A couple I know spend up to three hours a day meditating while holding down full-time jobs. Another friend rises before dawn everyday to pray, read the Bible and have her "quiet time" before beginning her day's work.

While her family sleeps, she studies and prays in the dark, depriving her-self of much-needed rest in order to satisfy a deeper requirement. All these transmutations of self-identity, energy, values and commitments are quite normal, potentially wholesome and life-affirming—both for the self and, as we shall see, for the greater good.

A reader wrote to say he identified with the profile of spiritually emerging adults that he read about in my first book:

> I have no checkbook, one credit card, and minimal clothes; reading makes up the bulk of my "social life." I have very little furniture, no radio in my car and few friends. I've consciously chosen to live like this as it makes me happy. My simple life brings contentment. I have, and do, experience both social and self-transcendence.

Not everyone wants or needs to live so austerely. But for those who do, getting to such a life is no mean trick. Thankfully, love paves our way.

◊ ◊

2. FROM PERSONAL SELF
TO UNIVERSAL SELF

———————— ◇ ————————

He who loves brings God and the world together.

Martin Buber

Actualizing spiritual potential involves, in some way or another, pulling back from society in order to view it—and ourselves—with detachment. This withdrawal may be perceptual. Or, it may involve long range, fairly permanent physical readjustments. In this *social transcendence*, we enter the wilderness of our own interior life. Now we awaken to our own limits, shortcomings and illusions, begin to spot our fictions, avoidances and childish sides. We see how we avoid full aliveness or responsibility. Perhaps we begin to appreciate our strength and decency. All this involves not merely analyzing ourselves (as in psychoanalytic treatment). It means transcending our small, egoistic self, tangibly, correcting our life wherever it falls short.

Then too, we may dissolve into a boundless, oceanic consciousness. This is self-transcendence, a second major value of our spiritual emergence. As we grow objective and mindful of ourselves and our times (society, culture, family patterns), our personal abilities are enhanced. As we tap into the deepest wellsprings of our own consciousness, we are infused with a new life. This means, over time, we regain awareness of who we are—recover directly our life's sacred reality and purposes.

Value shifts, the growth of self-respect and personal dignity, the introduction of specific interpersonal boundaries or ground rules and high work and behavioral standards are born as we develop spiritual intelligence. It is as if, synergistically, our personality—which Jung termed the supreme realization of the innate idiosyncrasy of a living being—becomes intuitively bright and knowing. This occurs, for the most part, slowly, as a gradual, incremental transmutation of consciousness. This is a move toward God-consciousness which also requires us to bid farewell to our limited self—the self with eyes that see not and ears

that hear not. For some this separation is fraught with fear, pain and turmoil. For others it is but another graduation, a stage along a converted
path wherein self is subordinated to a sacred, cosmic life.

Freedom is an important value of our movement toward the reborn
state. One person wants freedom to revise her use of time. She aspires to
be a productive contributor in her family or community and realizes that
she wastes her abilities by delays or artificial structures in her day. In
order to satisfy her goal, she seeks to upgrade her entire mode of operation. She must learn to tolerate frustration, manage her attention, become an autonomous, independent and resourceful thinker.

Someone else finds certain social activities now drain his energy. He
inches away from anything superficial. For him, freedom means the
chance to use his leisure as he sees fit. Soon, with his more focused,
intelligent management of time, he finds whole days and evenings are
liberated for reflective or creative projects. Another strives for personal
liberty (what the Hindus call "moksha": emancipation from worldly concerns) by cutting back on needless accumulation of goods or automatic,
impulsive spending.

When our love of freedom is coupled with a desire for stewardship
(i.e. the responsible care and management of our own and others' interests), our spiritual brightness is increasing. However, these intelligent
redirections of attention can trigger anxiety. Here and now a mighty
struggle between our new and old selves may ensue.

A businessman said that, at fifty-five, he finally got the courage to
ask for early retirement. Then, on the heels of his excitement, he was
practically overcome with fear. He saw that stepping into this revised,
more fulfilling life meant not so much material loss as the loss of his old,
false self—along with all the old, emotional baggage he'd carried for
years:

> All my life, I've been hung up on security issues, catastrophiz-
> ing, seeing myself living in a hovel. But I'm changing—lately I
> go forward, despite occasional bouts with fear. Freedom to
> express myself is essential for me.

> Earlier this year, I listed [and prioritized] my governing values.
> Love was my number one value, then came freedom—even
> ahead of character and health. I want to give something worth-

while to others, from within myself, and that's love. And I can only do that if I pay attention to this indwelling push to be myself—to pursue one thing over another. And that's freedom.

A lone decision, however logical or well planned, moves anyone into the unknown and therefore into inner turbulence. Society provides little support for such deep and substantive personal revision in adulthood. Years of studying the values and needs of the spiritually emerging adult tells me three steps must be taken if communities want to encourage responsible, spiritual maturity in adults. These include:

◊ Evolving languages and new relational models that support spiritual growth and development.

◊ Training spiritually aware therapists, including a sensible curriculum in graduate schools of counseling.*

◊ Providing general education in the restructuring of personal reality—in the process and intricacies of *metanoia* (conversion). (This too, as a core course, must assume a rightful place in the psychotherapeutic tradition and schooling of counselors, especially spiritual directors.)

On both the individual and community level, the world seems headed toward spiritual commitment and self-healing. The global ecology movement is one example of widespread environmental healing that has spiritual ramifications: As we grow sensitive to the sacredness of our own life, we realize that *all* life—animal, plants, indigenous cultures—is sacred, intertwined, unitive. Shifts in collective consciousness are usually gradual and depend on individual awareness being heightened, cultured and transformed. This takes time, energy and, simultaneously, happens out of time.

---

*To sample the thinking of a new breed of spiritually aware professionals, read Dr. C. Hageseth, *Thirteen Moon Journal* (Berwick), or Gary Toub, "The Usefulness of the Useless," in *Meeting the Shadow* (Tarcher).

The Growing Pains of Spirituality

During the incremental advances of personal growth, we can feel a host of growing pains—much as children and adolescents do. While the growing pains of early childhood are largely physical, and while adolescents ride a vibrant emotional roller coaster, spiritually evolving adults experience *all* of these: physical, psychic and spiritual jolts. This may stimulate what scripture calls the "groanings of the spirit."

At its deepest core, spiritual emergence is an infinitely rich and joyful movement. In practical experience, the journey is often complexly painful. As we move into our ambiguous future, we have no blueprints for living. We must live by faith alone. Then too, we feel a variety of new emotions. Even a cursory examination of the lives of those we consider saintly reveals personal turmoil. Reading Gandhi's notebooks or Dag Hammarskjöld's personal diary we get some sense of how heightened sensitivities or deep, delicate shades of feeling tear at those who have a spiritual conscience. On the surface, these lives appear normal, even emblematic of vital leadership or enviable productivity. Yet disturbing self-questions are natural precursors to the dying of the former self. For example, in Hammarskjöld's *Markings* (the spiritual journal that he called "my negotiations with myself concerning God"), we see how one great man was plagued by contradictory pulls. Despite fame, acclaim and enormous achievement he felt insecure:

> 'To listen'—in faith—to find one's way and have the feeling that, under God, one is really finding it again.

> This is like playing blindman's buff: deprived of sight, I have, in compensation, to sharpen all my other senses, to grope my way and recognize . . . [what] I would have known all the time was there, had I not blind-folded myself.[1]

The lamentations of the psalmists seem typical of this insecurity as they express all sorts of pain: sickness, community suffering and false accusation. The Davidic psalms are full of examples of personal distress. They ask God how long he will keep himself hidden or withhold his blessings.[2]

With similar insecurity we may examine our life, feel our pain or ask ourselves how much time we have left. We might nitpick at ourselves or hold ourselves accountable to a largely idealized, even rigid, standard of perfection that humans weren't meant to achieve (at least not in their mortal, "natural" state of mind).

Moving from the personal to the universal self (i.e. to final integration) does not mean losing identity, but rather gaining greater definition. This true individuality calls for rejection of all those outmoded, narrow forms of life which do not serve our elevated inward state. The universal self continually surrenders itself to love, not in the sense of restrictive or slavish one-on-one connectedness, but in rarefied giving of ourselves in contribution, service, devoted and disciplined acts. Only the exceptionally sane, hearty and faithful succeed. I do not mean to discourage. If we know we lack emotional stability or common good sense, competent spiritual direction is a must.

Parents who sacrifice personal comfort or goals to insure the enduring self-sufficiency of their children are one example of this need to love and contribute. A salesman I know longs to be a writer. Instead he devotes himself to paying the bill for his five children's college education:

> The day will come when my wife and I can live more simply and creatively. Right now we're both committed to putting our children through college. You have no idea how expensive this is, how hard all of us—even the kids—are working. But this is important to our family, to our futures, no matter what personal price we must pay.

Of course, this does not mean our sacrifice regards the other as an object, or that another person fulfills our own misspent, unexpressed life. To suggest this would mean that our love was narcissistically disturbed, possessive and controlling, served our own needs rather than the actualities of the other person's life.[3] If ours is a limiting love, then our compulsion to send a child through college (or do something equivalent for someone else) will lessen us as persons. On the other hand, the love that flows from the universal self expands our capacity to *be* and makes us more—not less—thankful and generous.

As we find voice for our actual needs we begin to realize our true life—however these expressions sit with other people. Dr. Alice Miller's treatment of this issue is worth mention: "From baby's cry to artist's creation" every authentic utterance is a sign that we are birthing our real life and its purposes. Especially if we were forbidden such vital expression in childhood (e.g. either punished for saying how and what we felt or over-shadowed by infantile, self-involved parents who needed our attention and care, who wanted us to be *their* mothers and fathers), then genuine self-disclosure produces much anxiety, even feelings of panic or death. Within our psyches we are dying. But this death involves only the demise of our small, artificially created self. And this is fine news for the "small death" that always precedes our birth into a larger, more animated self.

How do we know we are emerging spiritually? We feel inexpressible longing, perhaps for something we can't quite define. Despite complexity or weighty problems, we feel grateful to be alive. We experience peak (or ecstatic) instances. We feel the often illogical desire to be of service to others. We also gain strength for curbing our usual appetites (e.g., laziness or sloth), and find new enjoyment in fine art, liturgy, music, poetry or dance. All these feelings, drives and appreciations signal that a larger devotional life is on the rise.

Signs of Collective Spirituality

Thou hast led in thy steadfast love the people whom thou hast
        redeemed . . .
The peoples have heard, they tremble . . .

Book of Exodus

Our world seems to be going through a complex, basically good-natured adolescence. Spiritual development is like a coming of age. Collectively we do seem to be gradually discovering our fidelities, our stable center, and core self. Individually, we search for values worth living—and dying—for. Perhaps we achieve some degree of vocational or relational integrity. Ultimately, as adults—as a world-community—we should reach completion, whatever specific commitments and expressions this entails within each person. On both the individual and collective level, the reaching-out for spiritual wholeness bears signs, gives cues.

First, we realize we are growing whole, as our awareness becomes unified or non-dual.[4] This means our sense of separateness dissolves, judgment lessens, love increases. We grow faithful to our highest standards and values as our alienation subsides. Perhaps certain prejudices fall away. Or, our good humor increases—for "no reason" we feel happy, want to play or take vacation. Our intuition develops or we notice ourselves using under-utilized talents. We pursue new interests in a desire to be more well rounded. Inner peace also accompanies this turn toward full psychological health: firm self-identity; a strong, healthy ego; high self-esteem and the trait that Erik Erikson calls "fidelity"—the ability to sustain loyalties freely pledged in spite of the inevitable contradictions of value systems.[5]

Psychologically healthy people stick to their unique, perhaps idiosyncratic life plans and values as best they can. In spite of real or potential conflicts with the world at large, they tenaciously live their authenticity even if this means incurring personal discomfort, criticism or feelings of vulnerability. Increasing independence and *visible* uniqueness are key characteristics of spiritual growth. It is one thing for us to attend church regularly or say we believe in God, quite another to live at the intuitive edge of our faith.

Social and Self-Transcendence and Giving of Self

My research and interviews with self-actualizing adults reveal that these people tend toward both *self* and *social-transcendence*.[6] They possess at least some degree of that same unitive objectivity or self-forgetful consciousness experienced by artists, mystics and saints. I liken this mind to the non-attached, focused mind of the self-realized samurai, whose perceptual doors—as William Blake put it—have been cleansed.[7] Such persons have an inner, silent witness that discerns and thus undoes compulsions and bondage to prescribed responses or constricted ways of seeing.

Little by little, this watchfulness cuts us free from our illusory victim's script or our slavish dependence on the props or ceremonies of status, political power or dead rituals. Self-actualizing people tend to renounce automatic habits of convention or vanity in favor of spontaneity. Their smallest choices are made consciously and on the basis of well-thought-out standards. Because these choices are, by and large, autonomous, they may entail risk. At the same time, these choices release energy and human potential and are, in the main, exhilarating. One person describes how she nurtures her creative potential:

> I've played it safe in every area of my life. Slowly, I'm changing this—exploring my talents, not just in terms of leaving a behind-the-desk job but also in my dealings with people. I've

hidden in relationships, have kept quiet about feelings or opinions. As I experiment with all this in small-scale ways, I'm more alive, energized. The trick is to stay conscious, minute by minute, so as to catch my tendency to automatically, mindlessly act.

Illness may puncture our tendency to remain unconscious. One woman wrote,

> A year ago, around the time my husband and I separated, I got arthritis. I saw that I needed to make major improvements in my life. This has meant gradually looking for ways to live positively instead of destructively as I used to. You can't imagine all the ways negativity seeps into your thinking and behavior if you're not careful.

As we have seen, self-actualizing adults increasingly give of themselves from the wellsprings of their universal self. These actions may appear selfish—like the person who devotes hours to a community project while neglecting certain prescribed family chores or obligations. Such individuals *need* to contribute to others (or toward the greater good) more than they need material rewards, status or even family affection and approval. This need nags at them. If not addressed, it can create frictions and dissatisfactions in their seemingly secure comfortable relationships.

A friend told me that now his greatest satisfaction comes from recording tapes for the blind. He, like other spiritually emerging adults, gives up more profitable or sociable interests to honor this larger, caring side of himself. Now an impersonal, compassionate love requires him to withdraw time and personal attention from one interest in order to devote himself to another. This love is easily misunderstood and often disruptive. One individual may leave a posh job to spend quality time with family, another leaves family to work freely and without interruption in some larger context.

These separations illustrate love's universal force and outreaching quality. Gandhi's writings provide us with rich sources of information if we want to examine how the life of a *bramacharya* (monk) might alter our usual habits. Gandhi led an isolated life (despite marriage and a family), remaining celibate and fasting frequently. He arrived at this way of life by "gradual evolution, every step thought out, well considered and taken with the greatest deliberation."[8]

When people don't know "why" their love's outreaching, disciplining impulse makes them want to change their life, they can feel confused, torn apart by conflicting values. As a result, counterfeit marriages, hypocritical friendships and dysfunctional family ties may be undone and abandoned.

This undoing, when understood, can be resolved in common-sense fashion and then handled, if not painlessly, at least understandingly by the individual. Such was the case of a businessman whose increasing spirituality tugged at him for decades before he was able to articulate its charm and magnetic draw. His life's softer side required years of attention before comprehension came. He read about the subject, thought deeply about what was happening to him and went on numerous religious retreats. Self-study apparently let him see what he needed to do next:

> I'm 57 and I've decided to take an early retirement. This move excites me. Something tells me that my best times are ahead. I guess I'm one of a growing number of adults who realizes there's more to life than chasing a buck. I see I don't have to end my life controlled by the same notions that I started with.
>
> At this point, I've turned my mind to what I call my "higher values"—to service and to time spent in non-striving, non-exploitive ways. I couldn't have chosen this before—although I had a nagging sense of what was ahead of me.

Others face equally serious but different contradictions. One woman said:

> I lost my way when I went to a psychiatrist to help me decide "how" to achieve the goals I already knew were my own. He decided that I must be *cured* of my goal of being self-supporting, because "normal" women want marriage. I also knew that as a prayerful-type, I could only marry someone with similar inclinations or values.

This "fantasy," as my psychiatrist called it, was proof to him of my unwillingness to face reality (*his* version of reality). Now, with years wasted and so much to do, I seek a different brand of therapy—one that supports my spirituality as well as my more ordinary life goals.

What are the psychological characteristics of spiritually emerging societies? Spiritually mature societies demonstrate high regard for all life. People in such cultures perceive a universal interconnectedness among all living systems—plant, animal and human. What is termed unitive consciousness in the individual has its exact counterpart in the expanded collective awareness of a populace. So-called "primitive" or nature-based cultures like native American groups may have fit this profile; today's post-industrial societies seem a very long way from this ideal.

Fortunately, even a superficial survey reveals a current spiritual renaissance. We see evidence of greater sensitivity to the needs of the environment, to dying and to quality-of-life issues, and to improving personal practices of health or human relationships in general. There is, worldwide, heightened interest in animal, children's or victim's rights and increased ethical and moral sensibilities.

Only time will tell if this rising concern is substantive, or whether public commitment to community or human needs is only temporary.

Certain practices do seem to be changing for the better. For instance, just a few years ago public awareness to the downside of cigarette smoke was almost nil. Now all major airports, restaurants, civic buildings and workplaces either ban smoking entirely or have special locations where smokers may light up. Dietary habits have shifted toward lighter, leaner fare. People try to save money (rather than automatically consuming or accumulating debt). Polls report that Americans now give greater amounts of time to family life and do more volunteer work (39% in 1987; up 12% in ten years).

It is also true that adults must work harder today at their jobs just to "keep up." Surveys indicate that leisure time is down in middle-income America and that the term "middle-income" itself is changing. Fewer families meet national income averages than did twenty years ago.[9] More and more, both parents work; an entire generation of "latch key" children come home from school to empty homes. These harsh facts of life illustrate that to live effectively adults must find (or create) novel routes to personal freedom—especially if they want time for family, a personal life or a spiritual quest. Appropriate reading, journal work or support groups for these issues are helpful tools to sort out and shift priorities.

We need strength to make the tough choices that spiritual growth demands. Typifying this sort of strength, one person turns down a promotion because he does not want to relocate his family. Another debates whether to decline a move into upper management. She worries that corporate advancement will mean time away from her newly adopted child. A third decides to take an early retirement so that he can devote himself fully to volunteer work. All these issues have spiritual considerations that affect the individual's decision-making process. As we mature into our spiritual interests, we realize that it *is* possible to merge practical considerations with intangibles like love, service or personal fulfillment. One woman described how she reconciled her values with the necessities of her life:

> I've been a secretary for years and have hated it, although I'm successful. My divorce and my need to feed three children determined how I'd work.

> For a while now I've been thinking about personal satisfaction. As I mature, it's harder to stay in an environment where I'm pretending to be happy. Lately, I've been struck by the idea that as long as I must work, I might as well prepare for a truly contributive role in society. This role takes time to come into its own. So I suppose none of my past is wasted.

Traditional Institutions and the Growth of Spirituality

There are many ways, all inventive and bold, by which society can sustain its institutions. For instance, today's typical marriage is ripe for active, creative overhauling. Some men and women have already expanded their options with support groups and political action networks to educate and protect their rights or learn new ways of relating. In this, they are catalysts serving long-term community stability. Mr. Mom and Ms. Chairman of the Board show other adults "how" to reconfigure everyday life. They give themselves permission to stretch into more authentic ways of being and enable others to do the same. The numbers of men who stay home to actively raise children are growing. So are the "pioneers" who meet, in supportive settings, to reflect on their feelings of choosing new priorities. Women now represent the bulk of working class America. Institutions that fail to keep pace with the spirit and rise of individual awareness seem doomed.

Today's adults regularly leave long-standing responsibilities (marriages, careers, communities) to embrace new ones. They divorce, they move frequently, they arrange sabbaticals from career obligations or retire early. The midlife "crisis" is now seen as an expected, socially sanctioned time of self-inquiry rather than a shameful avoidance of responsibility.

What seemed in the 1950s to be mere faddish interest in therapy is now a full-blown branch of the health-care industry. "Recovery" programs like Twelve-Step, Overeaters Anonymous, and Adult Children of Alcoholics address every conceivable personal problem. Their premise is that we can't heal if we are ill at ease (dis-eased) with ourselves, and that growth and healing also mean we must forgive those who have hurt us in the past.

Personal sacrifice and living an examined, aware life are not instant achievements. Can adults, in a quick-fix society that quests for easy answers, endure in this commitment? Our answers depend largely on how each of us envisions (or relates to) God, or to what some simply think of as a "higher self." Incredible variations in individual experience will be found: one person easily tires of meditative or prayerful reflection but enjoys the solitary time spent in running or driving; another hungers for radical self-transformation so that life is forever altered; a third wants no part of the subject of spirituality at all. The rare person, still in the minority, steps out, over time, into an ineffable, unexplainable reality. Several characteristics show us that we are moving along more spiritual lines:

◊ Our desire and capacity to serve others increases.

◊ We grow willing to correct certain personal flaws (or limitations) like lack of restraint, over-indulgences, or avoidances.

◊ Our interest in spirituality deepens: God, afterlife, questions like "Who am I?" concern us. We enjoy reading the Bible or books that have a mystical, supernatural theme.

◊ Our creative drives, intuition and spontaneity develop.

What would make people answer a radical interior summons that could separate them from others, that wrests them from a secure and conventional life? Whatever this broad ineffable something turns out to be, when we are rightly called, we gain more—not less—purity of heart, grace and broad affection. Each individual ultimately must wholly identify with this, this stirring of love—there are no half-ways, pretendings or compromises in the authentic spiritual quest.

◊ ◊

3. RESISTING OUR GOOD

———————— ◊ ————————

Though one believe in the Law, he will rarely practice it; for people are engrossed by pleasures. Gautama, be careful.

Janist Sacred Narrative

Over a decade ago I redesigned my life in order to elevate the quality of both my contemplative and corporate life. I saw others before me who had managed this, and they seemed far better off for their achievement. Also, I watched many corporate clients struggling to shape their lives along the same grounded but non-conventional lines. Countless people whom I interviewed for various research projects did the same.

My corporate clients are influential, well-educated and financially secure. They do not conform to the stereotypical image of either the corporate boor or the mystical misfit. Nonetheless, as early as 1975 I heard what seemed confessions of people's interior or religious urgings. These matched what I too had felt for many years. People were exploring whether to take seriously these curious promptings of spirit. One sensitive executive described his perceptual shift this way:

> I've effectively used my mind and society's demands to avoid any real connection to myself. Suddenly my intelligence blossomed: I saw I'd been living in what amounted to one dimension since childhood. Images of what I thought were a "happy childhood" began reappearing—this time with sharp, objective accuracy: I faced up to my deceased father's alcoholism, his self-inflicted pain (ultimately his death) and my own twisted upbringing.

> I liken my awakening to the revolution in Eastern Europe: Myths and repressions are overthrown as I search for new ways to see myself, to work and just to be.

43

My forte is fiction writing. But I'm currently in charge of budg-
ets and fiscal affairs for a huge bureaucracy. I don't yet have the
courage to leave a position with so much power and status—
but I'm getting ready, however long this phase takes.

Over time and with the accumulation of scores of comments like
these, I realized that not only was it possible, it was *essential* that adults
actualize their highest standards, ideals and animating essences within
the context of a practical, otherwise "worldly" life. Apparently others
agreed. Many adults experience similar urgency and concretely step out
to satisfy their elevating self-view and their mind's mystical expansion.

One CEO spends a period of silence at a Quaker retreat he's heard
about. The experience renews his creative life. A corporate attorney
sheepishly tells me about wanting to create a self-sufficient farm in Idaho
or Wisconsin and move there permanently with his family. (To my
knowledge, he is still working on this plan and keeps the idea to himself.)
A doctor in a successful group-practice confesses she's always wanted to
be an artist but has never received any encouragement from family or
mentors. She now studies art while maintaining her practice.

These examples still are, I think, the exception. Many people yearn
for truer, more authentic ways of working and living but have no ready
answers when I ask them why they don't encourage themselves along the
vocational and spiritual lines they'd most prefer. Nevertheless, they feel
they are wasting their lives in some essential way and, more significantly,
that their delays thwart or sin against themselves. One person drinks to
excess to forget his boredom; another tries to find stimulation and escape in promiscuity. Another, more intelligently, reads everything available on related, self-development subjects as a way to find out what steps
to take next.

At the same time that I began to hear these disclosures from my
corporate clients, I observed numerous people actualizing what author
Duane Elgin calls "voluntary simplicity." They lived in an "outwardly
simple and inwardly rich" way.[1] These were, for the most part, individu-
ating adults who granted me interviews. Of all ages, types and backgrounds, these people serve as vivid examples of America's growing
spirituality. Since my early interviews (in the late 1970s and early 1980s),
I have received testimonials from all over the world that reinforce the
idea that it is possible (perhaps not easy) to live authentically while

emerging into a peak or unitive state, while growing into one's fully integrated, transcendental self.

Compromises and Resistance

Although spirituality is a fact of life for many contributive but otherwise non-"religious" adults,[2] other adults remain totally stuck. Perhaps people fear and are ill-prepared for their good. Like the person quoted above, they too feel, "I don't yet have the courage to leave ..."— not realizing that transmuting a circumstance does not always mean abandoning it.

In part, this ill-preparedness is *resistance*: a usually unconscious set of symptoms by which we stave off, repress, delay or withhold certain unacceptable wishes, goals, activities or ideas. Freud's writings indicate that this phenomenon includes a strategic, meaningful constellation of symptoms called *compromise formations*. Our repeated acts of repression, withholding or delay mean, in psychological lingo, to *"balance anxiety and guilt of the conscious personality against the pleasurable gratification sought by the unconscious."*[3]

In other words, our past trauma or conditioning causes us to selectively substitute symptoms for growth. We delay our progress toward intimidating goals by our preoccupations. For example, we may unconsciously use negative feelings, say fear, to undermine our professional success. We feel anxious about a promotion and therefore turn it down or fail a test. Perhaps we recoil from our true objective, thinking that our goal is beyond us or too dangerous. We may "use" confusion or uncertainty or childish behavior or poor judgment in similar ways: to thwart ourselves. As we approach our goals, we might alternate any assortment of symptoms and repeat this unproductive pattern.

On the other hand, by increasing our spiritual brightness we develop a natural wisdom (a mind/body, supra-knowing). This then gradually enables us to transcend our formerly imprisoning symptoms. Here and there we begin to behave effectively. Somehow, over time, we solve old problems or actualize our dreams. We learn to complete things, or (instead of blaming ourselves for our inabilities to take this or that step forward) we simply invest time in building interior strength. The following paragraphs explore this issue generally; later chapters return to it more fully.

Fear of the Good as Resistance

> Make excursions in pure simplicity. Identify yourself with non-distinction. Follow the nature of things and admit no personal bias. Then the world will be in peace.
>
> > Chuang Tzu, Taoist sage

Many people live with debilitating anxieties about the very changes they know will help them thrive and flourish. I interpret this as a fear of life. This is what Krishnamurti must have meant when he wrote that some people cannot love because they are afraid to feel utterly helpless. As love and life are inseparably linked, if we cannot *love* (or live in its deepest sense) it is because our vulnerability is too great; we are then inordinately anxious about loss of intimacy.[4,5]

The onset of spiritual growth means we move out into love and into our life despite our nameless, quite real apprehensions. Some do this, as did the thirteenth century Sufi poet Rumi, by falling in love with a distant goal—in his case, full self-realization. Desire gave Rumi the energy and drive to love in this manner. Others fall in love with another person. They grow in (and because of) a marriage or parental relationship. A sound, affectionate marriage or the birth of a beloved child can initiate us, start our personal journey into selfhood. For those who were abused (physically or emotionally) as children, the step into final integration may seem almost impossible although wholeness is craved more than any other goal.

People continually tell me that they dearly want to change their situations. Some want to leave their nine-to-five jobs to spend more time with family or in some specific, meaningful work. (This morning as I was writing a scientist called and said that he'd like to start his own research business, but fears economic hardship.) Others, who have never been married (or who have never even loved anyone), long for marriage and a stable, special relationship. Single women who don't want to marry but who do want children frequently sound like this:

> I want to adopt a child, have seen my attorney and know that I have the psychic and physical strength to do this. I believe my right livelihood is parenting—but I'm terrified of leaving my job, the benefits, the security. Even though I think I'd be able

to set up a modest business in my home, I can't get off the dime. Any suggestions?

I regard this sort of stuckness not as sin, crime or cowardice but merely as resistance, as lack of readiness. Our fears—or resistances—can be healthy signs, telling us to go slow, proceed with caution. Our temporary solution might be to find some tangible, lesser ways to prepare ourselves for our goals, while controlling our tendency to brutalize ourselves with self-criticism or pressure for our under-development and delays. Moving forward gradually does not mean we'll *never* get what we want. Resistance is often a sign that we are not ready yet for the life or objectives we want.

Otherwise competent, high-achieving adults easily get confounded when they're lacking some "X-quality" (or characteristic) that they can't name. They see others achieving something they dearly want but can't figure out how they'll get it. Then they get discouraged. Usually what people want is liberation, but they give this different labels. Freedom from conflict, the ability to use their minds or talents fully, and love and belonging are all variations of personal freedom that somehow eludes them. Trapped in opposing currents, they sabotage or back away from their goal while still relentlessly pursuing it. One person, who consulted me on this, described such resistance:

> For years, I've rewarded myself for just getting through another day. I rely on alcohol at the end of every day to relieve stress generated by constantly coping with deep-seated feelings of inadequacy, and just to feel plain warm inside. This is now a major problem in my life. My inability to stop drinking reinforces my sense of no-control, low self-esteem and general unworthiness.

> Ironically, I'm slowly realizing that I'm engaged in a lifelong, lengthy process of redefinition, a process I can no longer postpone or ignore. At this time I weave back and forth, between my fears and addictive habits and my desire to move ahead healthfully.

If this individual pays attention to redefining herself and serves her growth patiently and responsibly, her addictive habit will wane. Eventually she'll manage it. This is when proper counseling helps.

A friend desperately craves a personal relationship to "get her needs met." By this she means she wants unconditional love. This, she feels, will satisfy her inner hunger.

I sense a deeper need: She has yet to love, or unconditionally accept, herself. Lacking that, all attempts to build relationships will flounder. Her interpersonal strategies are counter-productive: she tries to extract compliments from people, grab attention or receive guarantees about her friends' unending devotion or her lover's willingness to give her lifelong security. The intimacy she craves will come after she learns to support her own life, to love herself and others. This woman should start smaller, identify (through therapy and certainly through self-study) the elementary steps by which she herself can satisfy her more basic needs and build spiritual maturity. To reach out for the larger goal (i.e. of a permanent love-relationship) seems like trying to read Shakespeare without first having grasped the alphabet.

By contrast, another friend (an only child who had insensitive parents) realized he needed interpersonal and relational skills before he could have a fulfilling, lasting marriage. This in itself was a mark of spiritual growth and increasing acuity. Figuring out is a skill; it can be developed.[6] This man was smart in his initial objective: He figured out that striving for an idealized love-relationship was unproductive.

He'd never shared anything before: not toys, not time, not himself. He'd never learned how to speak about what he felt—couldn't even distinguish one feeling from another. His first goal was to live with another person for a year or more. He knew he wanted to relate on an elementary, less intimate basis as a start. He also had to confront those difficulties that previously presented themselves as insoluble problems in past relationships. Soon he mastered many key skills.

> At first, when I came home from work and found my room-mate in *my* living room, with his stuff on *my* coffee table and his CDs in *my* audio system, I would get angry. I felt encroached upon. I wanted my own space and privacy. Then, over the last year, I began to handle this: I'd talk about my feelings with him or work things out inside myself so that I reconciled myself to the realities of having a roommate.

> I can express subtle feelings—it's not impossible. Every step forward makes my relationship with my girlfriend and even my

co-workers that much better. For the first time, I'm optimistic about my future as a husband and father.

This is exactly how we build spiritual strength. First we identify the skills we need. Intuition, creativity, resourcefulness, inner peace are all spiritual goals. We start small, strategically plotting a path to our larger objective (however we name or phrase it). To wish prematurely for the ability to make full-blown religious commitments or have Abraham's level of faith or immediate, specific answers about ways to transform our daily life into a sanctified expression of devotion seems both childishly idealized and counter-productive. Our symptoms of delay mean that we aren't yet ready and that the spiritual objectives we have in mind are highly advanced. Barring instantaneous conversion, we may need to live, in everyday life, "as if" the kingdom of heaven were truly at hand while simultaneously meeting our mundane responsibilities. Moses, David, Joseph and even Jesus took time (in some cases years) to strengthen their inner capacities. Paying bills, "chopping wood and carrying water" give us ways to build our spiritual skill. In this matter, the Quakers, Shakers and Zen Buddhists have much to teach us.

Confusion and Unreadiness as Resistance

When our inner natures are underdeveloped, we intellectually muddy-up spiritual issues. Confusion can be a symptom of anxiety about getting our wishes met. One person admitted this: "I get confused when I think about spirituality. Those philosophical books my friends read make no sense to me." Another said, "I can't understand why I'm not able to find my life's answers. Even thinking about this is dumbfounding." Practically too, we may lack common-sense answers to help us meet our life's everyday demands. An enhanced inner life requires skillful, real-world action. If we're not ready, say, to leave a job or to simplify life or decline spirit-draining social activities or manage our time and resources more productively, then often our minds cloud over other next-step activities that could help us get to our goals. This seems a blessing in disguise, since it's very expensive (i.e. in terms of money, time, emotional wear and tear) to jump into something before we're fully prepared to make a go of it. In this instance, "slow and steady wins the race," as the tortoise found out in that old fable.

Until we're emotionally ready, mature spiritual growth eludes us.

Then we idealize this life. We don't realize that our imagination is but another impediment. An undisciplined, impractical mind keeps us running after some stupendous, exciting religious experience, which ultimately may turn out to be a huge fiction. Or we think we need a special cult to help us reach enlightenment. For example, people who express sore disappointment at life spent in cultic communities often return to their former life much wiser for this reason. Their experience reroutes them from the very opportunities (here and now) that could provide real spiritual advancement, namely, facing daily schedules and chores; sticking with commitment to marriage; raising a family; investing fully in a meaningful career. Routines give us opportunities to grow spiritually.

St. Paul's description of some people as more "noble-minded" than others underscores the theme of preparedness. When we're developmentally ready, our skills and our disposition (inner and outer) accomplish what we say we want. Then our desire for spiritual growth is matched by the capabilities we need to achieve our goal.

St. Paul reminds us that some otherwise fully grown adults remain as children, while others receive God's word "with great eagerness" and faithful study.[7] When we're ready we are receptive. Resistances fall away. Then we find our common sense answers and life flows again.

In the New Testament adults are often called babies—ill-prepared, unable to chew up the tough meat of spiritual truth. St. Paul makes it clear that moving from spiritual desire to action entails readiness. We *learn* to conduct ourselves properly; this does not come automatically. We *learn* to make good use of our time. We *learn* what it means to grow temperate, wise and thankful.[8] Ultimately we discover that desire alone is insufficient—actual hard work is necessary, as is grace. And grace comes in various ways. As we take steps to go from wish to wish-fulfillment, we feel some added power or capability.

We must not misguidedly assume that mature spirituality comes without a proper foundation of general psychological health. The sins of the fathers may be visited upon the sons, but there is nothing that says the offspring shouldn't use their free will and their intuitive, native abilities to move beyond these failings.

For instance, all normal, uncompleted psychological tasks of childhood and adolescence must be addressed as part of adulthood's psychic work. This often requires us to double-back, as it were, to heal or reconcile early pain and trauma, or to finish up what we started in youth but left undone. Erroneously, sometimes we imagine we can simply hop-skip-and-jump into self-realization. We may apply instantaneous, self-help methods to our bruised, frightened psyches or hope, magically, over a weekend workshop, that we'll reach Samadhi. This is improbable.

The qualities of love, forgiveness, interior calm or harmony are states of being that build incrementally, and then influence every shred of experience. These are not like galoshes we put on when our life's weather turns stormy. These facets of spirituality accompany self-discipline, the softening of a hardened heart and whatever gifts of grace we receive. Spiritual maturity comes in its own sweet time, certainly after we undertake some appropriate strivings and self-purification. Even Christ's disciples struggled to gain faith, healing skills and pure God-consciousness. Our initial strivings are based, partly, on knowing who we are, what we need, who we want to become and why we feel we must have these characteristics.[9] All these understandings must be folded into our ordinary, daily life.

As we live these comprehensions, we "strengthen hands that are weak and knees that are feeble."[10] Walking or talking, we grow whole. This movement heals limbs which were lame.[11]

Illustrating the wish for immediate psychic relief and spiritual maturity (in this case, peaceful reconciliation or forgiveness) is a woman who said that forgiveness "didn't work." She'd tried forgiving her family for making her the sole care-giver of her sickly, dying mother. But her pain and self-defeat lingered:

> I'm addicted to chewing bottles of aspirin. I eat up bottle after bottle of them. My hair is falling out. I'm disoriented. You'd think I'd stop since I'm getting physically ill. But when my mother's deteriorating Alzheimer and cancer act up, I'm back into the aspirins.

> I've been her only care-giver since my father died. My brothers and sisters won't help. I've tried writing out positive affirmations. I try to forgive specific family members, but I'm impatient. These things don't work.

If we sense our own coping skills are faulty, we must seek proper, long-term help, like therapy or ongoing talks with our physician. To skirt the obvious by trying instant, over-simplified methods is proof that we aren't applying intelligence to our life. Good judgment, appropriateness of the methods or advisors we seek, and our rational, reasoned thinking skills are all signs that we possess sound competency on which further growth, like spiritual health, will be built.

At around twelve years of age, emotionally healthy children easily exercise "as if" or logical thinking skills. They can reason their way out of amazingly complex problems. Many adults don't do as well. Their problem-solving effectiveness is a report card they must learn to read before properly diagnosing what they need to do next. If very young people can (and do) adopt rational coping ability (usually without formal instruction), then we, as adults, can learn to stop tripping ourselves up. Our own real-world, skillful means deserve attention. This means getting professional help, not hastily reading self-help books or living a fiction that says the world, not we, is out-of-step. Spiritual growth (including all its virtues) demands complete sanctification, which is to say the uprooting and correction of our weaknesses. "Without this no one will see the Lord."[12]

The opening of our way and these attributes come by virtue of grace and are some of the many "signs following" our faithful, active, reaching-out. Readiness gives our desire its holy life, its vitality. Then readiness makes it possible for us to complete the goal—because we have grown in both ability and understanding.[13]

Without readiness, achieving anything meaningful is virtually impossible. We must not give up in despair, but rather we just accept ourselves wherever we are now. Gradually, conservatively and with full trust, as we actively engage ourselves with the ideas and realities of the values and virtues we want, we receive the grace necessary to experience that very life. Swami Vivekananda's comment, "Why wait for heaven? Make it here," instructs us properly.

Whatever our present state, as we objectively examine our life we find practical actions needed to improve our minds or attitudes, our bodies or our home: cleaning a drawer; organizing the garage; phoning or visiting a friend; cultivating a rose garden—anything we do takes us to God if our thoughts and choices rest in his virtues.

Childishness as Resistance

It seems important to stay open to our childish qualities. As children, we thought, spoke, reasoned and behaved imperfectly. Just so, childish-adults are self-involved, dependent, inept or otherwise unwilling (and unable) to take responsibility for their lives (not simply in the conventional sense but in a spiritual one). If we remain receptive to our avoidances, we stand a good chance of correcting our obvious and willful self-sabotage.

Sometimes we flit from philosophy to philosophy, or start and stop our search for the unitive life. We meditate fiercely for hours on end, then abandon this practice because there is no instant reward or bliss. As spiritual infants we easily can exhibit the deer-caught-in-the-headlights syndrome: Faced with tough choices, we know our words (or next-steps) will make or break our well-being, but we become frozen and inactive. This is natural. We may remain inert or stay in what we know is the wrong job, friendships or habits for years. As we advance, our good calls to us. We know exactly what to say or do and are ready to accept the consequences.

The bridge from spiritual infancy to advancement can span a lifetime or just a short period. Here too, patient waiting is a spiritual victory. St. Francis of Assisi's comment that we should accept as a grace all the things—and people—who impede us from loving God perfectly underscores this notion. Although this seems a subtle point of instruction in obedience, what choice do we have? If we can't get something, or someone, out of our way, we may as well interpret the roadblock in the best, most favorable light until we can.

Lack of Self-Acceptance as Resistance

The less we hide from or fight our ignoble tendencies, the more likely it is that we will outgrow them. Patience and especially self-acceptance are signs that we are building strength. This is true not only in spiritual matters, but in physical terms as well. Children whose leg muscles are not ready for walking continue to crawl. Yet we do not berate small children for this. Generally, advancement comes at the precise point of our honest, non-judgmental self-acceptance. Our willingness to admit that we are human is a sign of humility and truthfulness. This brings spiritual enrichment. In other words, we become more fully human (instead of thinking we are demi-gods) when we admit our limits openly. Of course, in saying this, I do not mean that we should exaggerate our flaws, always attending to this or that vice so as to dominate conversation or have all minds on our situation. We gain a healthy "emptying" (or simply an interior balancing) by seeing ourselves and meeting each moment truthfully.

Self-acceptance paves the way for the realization that, on our own, we can do very little to change. When all is said and done, we need each other's help, and, most of all, we need to puncture that balloon of vanity that says we must be flawless. For this, trust in God, the Tao (Ultimate Reality), is primary: God's grace—not our own efforts or our blemish-free conduct—and his love are required for a sanctifying life.

St. Thérèse, known as "The Little Flower," wrote often of the way this self-acceptance, truth-telling, or humility renders us completely dependent on God:

> . . . let us take our place humbly amongst the imperfect, deem-ing ourselves little souls whom the good God must sustain at each moment. As soon as He sees us truly convinced of our nothingness and we say to Him: *My foot hath slipped; Thy mercy, O Lord, hath held me up* (Cf. Ps. 93:18), He stretches out His Hand to us; but if we will attempt to do something grand . . . He leaves us alone.[14]

Some people (particularly those who take great pride in their ability to control life's outcomes—e.g. health, finances, etc.) may be offended by such quaint or tender sentiments. But St. Thérèse's remarks, while ardent and emotional, seem no different than, say, Eckhart's vast, pro-found commentaries on emptiness. The Zen monk's goal is similar—to attain "don't-know-mind":

> A monk once traveled to a Zen master seeking advice on how to practice his discipline. The Master inquired, "Why did Bodhidharma come to China?" The seeker replied, "The pine tree in the front garden." Then the Master asked, "What does this mean?" Although the seeker grasped the essence of the koen, he couldn't verbalize a proper answer, so he said truth-fully, "I don't know." Upon which the Master said, "Only keep this don't-know mind. That is true Zen practice."[15]

In time, with a softened attitude, both our psyches and our material life (e.g. all the mundane, practical aspects of existence) can and should support our spiritual growth. We can gain the disposition and skill to move forward. This usually means our willingness to wait while, on the surface, nothing much changes.* This too seems all part of our inner work.

Feeling trapped, indecision, hubris or even the lack of skill or un-derstandable goals calls for one remedy: the building up of true interior strength. The high self-esteem or non-judgmental self-trust we want comes as we gain inner balance. This centeredness assists us in further translating our desires (and our own particular destiny, with its joys, hardships, responsibilities and commitments) into a viable spiritual exist-ence, a holy life. Along the way we may pass through likely phases. First, we feel a radical call or strange, dislocating urgency to improve our life. We can think of this as an "awakening"—as if an inner alarm goes off. Next comes our particular, quite personal response. Some people wait and wait. Others drop what they're doing and run for the nearest desert. Regardless of our response, this development can take years.

There are benchmarks to our unitive journey. We seek and gain self-discipline, inner skills, the desire to make substantive personal sac-rifices or live out our highest values. Our mature spiritual formation is furthered greatly by uplifting and corrective words, images and ideals. These help us recollect ourselves in God and gain real inner freedom— a life worth living. Sacred readings, silence, solitude and proper, holy identifications are all vehicles for this positive growth. It is to these sanctifying elements we now turn.

◊ ◊

---

*The later sessions in this book are designed to help with this "waiting."

4. IDENTIFICATION FOR REBIRTH

◇

He who knows does not speak.
He who speaks, does not know.

Tao Te Ching,
Self-Training of the Sage

We don't huff-and-puff our way, willfully, into a reborn state. Neither do we succumb to negative introversions or make too much of our emotional ups and downs. Rather than forcing renewal (which we can't do anyway), rather than over-emoting, we can and eventually do ease up, learn to take things as they come. We begin to watch ourselves objectively to notice what authentic needs must be met and what artificialities can be dropped. Our chosen disciplines and meditations help change our minds, our hearts and our loyalties. These do not coax or bribe God into our corner. He is already there.

Most of all, we grow into the discovery that we must revise our identifications: Look away from limited beliefs and the materiality of our "old" person to those of our new, real self. This is key to union with the object of our love, that is to say, with God. And this seems the true purpose of all religions. Religion's varied forms and doctrines are meant to take us Home.

During this transition we learn humility. For some of us, this comes naturally; we may feel confounded to be so abruptly emptied of our former way of being. "It's like being stood upon my head," said one woman about the aftermath of an intense month of spiritual work. Another, a young student, who had read *Ordinary People as Monks and Mystics* while at a monastic retreat and then again in college, found that listening to his "inner man of the heart" was unsettling, even scary:

This is the most unusual aspect of my life to date. I feel an inevitable confusion and uncertainty. This feeling accompanies my every move forward (spiritually speaking) and I'm anxious.

It's an incredible comfort to know that these experiences are not unique to me and that they are, in fact, common to many who travel this path.

Here is precisely when prayer, reading, and reflecting on scripture and meditation can become our most valuable allies. Training our minds to turn in new directions takes some doing—especially in adulthood. Discussions with empathic friends or a spiritual director can also alleviate tension. We can feel radically summoned but not have a proper, appropriate response. As a start, we adopt less egocentric strategies than we used in the past. Instead of suppressing or over-controlling our spontaneous responses and instincts, we now wait patiently, watching for our best and truthful words or actions.

Active Non-Doing

These insights come more easily as we let go of effort and phoniness. Our mindful let-it-be attitude is not passivity; we are active, watchful, alert. This can be exhausting. In the beginning, it's hard to stay awake and focused all the time. Erich Fromm generously treats this matter of concentration (and love—which is yet another side to this issue) in his book, *The Art of Loving*:

> Concentration is by far more difficult to practice in our culture when everything seems to act against the ability. . . . The most important step . . . is to learn to be alone with oneself without reading, listening to the radio, smoking or drinking. Indeed to be able to concentrate means to be able to be alone with oneself—and this ability is precisely a condition for the ability to love.[1]

I am, of course, not suggesting a bug-eyed, forced attention—simply the growth of full, objective awareness. The Zen Buddhists call this a big mind/open mind. This mind houses that large love spoken of earlier and also life, potency and our creative energies.

Paradoxically, during this training period (which can last a lifetime) we need more, not less, activity—but of a special, organizing type: quieter, less fussy tasks help order our thinking in this time of potential confusion. We are becoming vigilant caretakers of our minds, our speech and our everyday, ordinary choices. Our goal now is to repossess "that self which we truly are."

We are, after all, disciplining ourselves toward authentic, whole personhood. Our objective asks us to be faithful to a new, high and personally elegant standard of thought and behavior—one specifically our own (and probably imprinted in our DNA). No one has our blueprint for what to do. Nor can we copy-cat someone else's solutions. We must get out of our own way and live non-interferingly with our growing refinements and life-affirming instincts. In this way we release our newly born, animating essence from the prison of suppression which we ourselves had engineered.

One well-regarded community leader knows that he undermines himself by consistently letting people and circumstances define his day and his life:

> I set goals, only to drift away from them if something "better" comes along. I announced my leave of absence from work only to change my mind when an interesting project was offered to me.

Another person needs to "be" somebody. A hunger for status and prestige motivates her career choices and social priorities:

> A gold embossed business card; titles; an invitation to the "right" dinner parties; a large, well-polished desk and VIP treatment by others—these are my toys; these drive my ambitions. Lately however, such baubles have less attraction for me. I want deep, meaningful accomplishments. But before I reach for these, I feel it necessary to erase the appeal of all this glitz from my life. Problem is, I don't know where to start.

The ability to express our honest, unvarnished concerns may mark a turning point in our bid for an authentic existence. For years, I held in anger and behaved according to protocols I'd learned were proper. This cost me. My natural energy seeped out here and there anyway, like blood from an imperceptible cut. But, for the most part, I remained soft-spoken, undemanding, eternally polite. Not until adulthood did I lose my temper or speak up excitedly for my own interests. This came only after I gave time and attention to my spiritual life. At first these outbursts unsettled me. But slowly I learned that anger is an arrow which, like pain, points the way to error. As writer Ruth Gendler says, "Anger is a meticulous reporter."[2] Self-expression, boldness and full-engagement are but variations of vigorous, loving aliveness.

This does not mean that spirituality encourages displays of temper or over-reactions of emotion. Quite the contrary: control comes in due course. A self-regulating richness of being, a non-self-conscious willingness to be known and unashamed of our "nakedness" also flourishes. By contrast, keeping our distinctive natures under wraps (concealing our likes, dislikes, our opinions and feelings) warps our life's full potency.

Essential Imperfection

It is dishonest to pretend perfection when it doesn't exist. With more complete development we control our tempers or our desires for praise and status. But we must first go through or cancel out, in a natural sequence of experiences, our need to please or impress others. Only then is self-control a virtue and not a vice of hypocrisy.

There is a story about a dull, unimaginative person who lacked all ambition and drive. One day this dullard encountered a famous guru and inquired what to do to find God. The guru, noticing the man's apathy, asked, "Can you lie?" "No," replied the man. "Then," said the guru, "you must learn how to do so. It is better to tell a lie than to live as a dead weight, a piece of wood. At present you are too dull even to do something wicked. The highest state (beyond all activity) is calmness and serenity. But you are simply inert." The guru meant that each must pass courageously through various, normal stages of being and meet his or her fears head-on before entering that state of perfect control or calmness known as nirvana or heaven.[3] In just this way, our spiritual wholeness arrives as we identify our limits and work bravely to surmount them. Over the years, as we pass through natural human barriers, we develop real skill to handle, then transcend, these problems. Then in truth (not as Pharisees, who fake their lofty state) we reside in real interior silence.

Learning to live with previously unexpressed parts of ourselves is like learning to live in the same house with a new intimate—a spouse, child or family member. Growth in this authentic relationship is integral to our spiritual maturity.

Unfoldment Includes Orderly Life in Society

This unfoldment meanders through somewhat distinctive stages, but growth is one seamless, continuing process. At first, for instance, we may just accept the fact that we are distinctive and that no one has our answers. We start thinking for ourselves, take chances in self-expression and daily choices. When and if we mimic someone we realize we're undermining our life and self-correct, returning to a less-known but more authentic way.

We move from "proper," automatic social adjustment to the use of our highest inner standard as a guide for conduct. This tendency accelerates as we approach a wholehearted change of mind and heart: *metanoia.* By this we transcend normal perception (including beliefs about our limited self) and society's logical norms.

Illumination always starts with our life in society. That is, self-realizing people are not anarchists (although they can feel an emotional, experiential anarchy taking place within). They are only caught in the throes of radical, personal interior change, becoming God's most whole and loved idea.

Full realization is impossible to gain without first receiving enculturation in society (which may, or may not, include indoctrination in a strict religion). However, we eventually outgrow it.

The dictates of enculturation let us go on automatic pilot. We behave within the law while transcending law. None gain final integration without moving, if only in consciousness, beyond themselves and the bounds of society. This is, in part, what self-and-social transcendence implies.

Dr. Aresteh suggests that without our first becoming, say, Confucianists and living in strict accordance with that social norm, we simply lack the proper foundation for becoming Taoists, liberated souls.[4] Similarly, Christianity, Judaism or Buddhism—or other religions—supply the symbolic and thematic scaffolding for our spiritual construct, our highest interior formation. These provide our mind with identifications for its sacred patterns, its heroic, holy images and ultimately its release. Without this, "in the natural" as evangelists say, our mortal mind lacks discipline for its ascent.

Fully illuminated Buddhists, for instance, accept their disciplines and devotions until they internalize the notion that the Buddha lives within. The well-known phrase, "If you see the Buddha on the street, kill him," is meant to further this awareness. Enlightenment brings the Buddhist embodiment of all the Buddha's traits and values and in some unfathomable manner provides a way to absorb his sacred essence. Realized Christians find Christ living within them in much the same way: Christ is a good shepherd, a lamb, the "model of perfection." The Holy Spirit becomes a person, a daily intimate, a real companion. Thus we find metaphors for our life's reconstructions and rebirth.[5]

Martin Buber wrote that the primary word—I/Thou—is spoken only as our whole being relates to I/Thou. This optimal, divine bond allows our small, egocentric self to experience union with God. Walt Whitman's lines (from what poem I don't know) "There was a child went forth every day, and the first object he looked upon, that object he became . . ." describes this very phenomenon. As we fall in love with our object of desire (i.e. God), as we achieve fusion with that love, we merge into and become that.

Proper identifications with selected precepts of our faith also help us in daily life.[6] I have heard that the Dalai Lama's interpreter is unflappable during busy, tedious tours. When asked how he remains so calm, he says that waiting (e.g. for the tour bus in small, cramped quarters) is like the bardo—the forty-nine days between death and rebirth (described in the Tibetan Book of the Dead).

Whatever our particular path, our specific religious practices are significant. Our religion is richly mind-shaping. Belief establishes our relationship with God. Liberated, we then move beyond belief into pure knowing.

As we become aware of our mysterious and inextinguishable inner force, we also seek ways to demonstrate its light and power. For this we intuitively find viable outlets that let us express this new reality and devote ourselves to its complete emergence.

I know a young peace activist who considers himself a naturalist, an agnostic and a humanist. I seriously doubt that he would be comfortable adopting the notion of a cosmic or universal God. Yet he has had peak experiences much like those described by saints, religious poets and artists. His church is the outdoors, nature and the planets. He says his religion is to walk softly, to leave a gentle footprint on the earth and to protect the environment. This man is a good steward—considerate and helpful, he serves others by working for world peace. His are, to me, holy goals. Gentleness, service, mildness and peace are all fruits of his spirit. Certainly his efforts for a non-violent world are grounded in charity. Another man, also unchurched, also highly spiritual, says, "I don't go to formal services on Sunday. I'm never out of church."[7]

Our spiritual expressions and the vehicles by which we elevate these (e.g. religion, prayer, meditation or chanting, readings, walks in nature, etc.) help us bond to whatever we sense to be beyond-self. This identification is a process by which we draw to ourselves the qualities of the object of our love, namely God. Incrementally we become like him, more his and less our own. Losing ourselves, we gain a new life. This rebirth is a systemic, experiential, total conversion.

Whatever words and constructs we use to explain this unfoldment, our spiritual perfection mirrors whatever (whomever) we gaze at or engage ourselves with. Over time, we integrate ourselves wholly with the object of our devotion.

This drive, or desire, seems of God. From the beginning, he exists. From the beginning, we are called and were, in fact, created exclusively for him. No doubt much (if not all) human misery comes from our misplaced and mistaken desire. Drug and alcohol addiction; promiscuity; yearning for bigger, better stimulations, are ways in which in error we attempt to reach beyond ourselves. Glamor, fame, sexual stimulation or flights of fancy and danger do seem, for a short time, to help us escape our ego's limits, but these false outlets lie to us. We were meant to experience a life beyond ourselves, to transcend our deprived, imprisoned states, but not chemically, nor through any worldly means.

When we finally figure out how to direct this drive productively, it seems impossible to speak of our discovery to others. Ordinary human words cannot describe our real motives, goals and subjective life. (Scripture promises that we shall learn to speak in "new tongues." We do need new tongues to communicate this inexplicable wish and its eventual experience; our usual languages do not suffice.)

We may also have peak (or ecstatic) spiritual experiences. These compound our frustrations of trying to live a spiritually relevant life in a world that is, at best, skeptical of Ultimate Reality. Peak experiences are highly charged; they integrate us still further—even uplift us. But they are, simultaneously, ego-shattering occasions which leave us picking up the fragments of our former identity, turning it this way and that, to see if our self-view is still intact. It isn't.

Beginning To Change Our Mind

During the early stages of spiritual evolution, before we discover what identifications might sustain our growth, we may find ourselves living in an upside-down fashion. No longer faithful to our normal life, not yet established in the new, we may wonder what will come of us. We may notice long-standing depressions, resentments or stalemates and realize we've had these companions for decades. One woman said that, as she gained deeper understanding of herself, she found that long ago, she lost her love of life:

> I'm searching for a lost love. Not a love for another person, but an appreciation or gratefulness for just being alive.

> Going from knowledge and understanding to actually taking steps to make needed repairs in my psyche is most difficult for me. Once I gather up my courage and make a corrective choice, I see it's the easiest thing I can do—so much easier, and more natural, than trying to live against myself. This work takes practice.

Our change can be either imperceptibly or dramatically stimulated by a sudden crisis or powerful reverential experience. Illness and loss force many of us to reconsider how we are living.

Each awakening instance assigns us much work. We must align our conscious life with our expanded insights. At the same time we sense that there is nothing much to do. Maharishi Mahesh Yogi says we gain the feeling that "Mother is at home"—a deep inner peace and consolation that stretches awareness beyond its present norms. Inner dimensions of safety—spurred by the experience of divine love perhaps—console us so that now we want to drop certain self-protective strategies (like working at the wrong jobs or marrying for the wrong reasons).

Meaningful and life-shaping though these peak instances might be, to wait for, or attempt to court, these all-consuming moments seems counter-productive. On the other hand, our here-and-now presence, our genuine thankfulness, that flows from these bursts of whole-seeing (and the practical choices these suggest) can and do further spiritual maturity.

Growth of Spontaneity

As we progress, we realize that *forced* union with the divine is impossible and that we will not reach enlightenment by checking off a lengthy "to do" list. We do not scrub, wash and launder our way into God's presence in order to merit transformation. We are hindered by too much concern to "improve," or to have this or that direct experience. (It is interesting that Buber called Satan "the hinderer.")

As we become receptive to our own interior silence and to the nuances and gifts of grace, we sense that growth into God is inevitable and that this union has always existed. St. Augustine, speaking to God, said, "You were with me, and I was not with you." Nor would we desire him if we were not wanted first. After all, it is God's love for us that awakens our need to find our way Home.

It can be thought strange to admit that we have spiritual experiences. For example, when someone is involved in a community or a corporate meeting or having dinner out with friends, light-hearted conversation is the norm. Most of us have little occasion for deep, trusted dialogue with others. As spontaneity and naturalness increase we want such dialogue and may even, in childlike simplicity, blurt out our state of mind or our goals. Perhaps one reason for the rise of adult support groups is that personal, fragile topics can be discussed safely and with dignity. As individual spirituality increases, our mainstream popularity may decrease. As we fix our eyes on God or turn our attention to simplifying and ordering life, we can become bores. Often it is prudent and necessary for us to pull back, go within or "drop out." Family and friends—perhaps even, as mentioned, psychological or helping professionals—easily misinterpret this.[8] In time (always in time, since real spiritual growth is a long-term, life-long process) if we tend toward wholesomeness, are guided properly and blessed with good judgment, we "drop back" in at an even deeper level of relatedness, social contribution and commitment than before.

Withdrawal and Self-Questioning

Shams of Tabriz (the Sufi poet Rumi's mentor, friend and teacher) was considered a fully self-realized man. Restless, after years of study, he traveled freely, questioning other enlightened scholars of his day to determine if his experience was truly authentic. At that point Shams extricated himself from the rule of all authority, traditions, and the entire scope of conventional life. Eventually he entered a self-imposed exile until, to his satisfaction, he reached complete personal transformation. In time he met Rumi and powerfully influenced the course of the poet's life. (Their discourses—Maqalat—have been published.) Shams is an extreme example of a common pattern of human spiritual development. Many ordinary people strain to keep themselves rooted in a busy, conventional life, while keenly longing for a solitary, simple way of being. Their pain might be lessened if they knew that such emotions are natural and if they could find mentors for their own spiritual journey.

Although we need not drastically disrupt our present life, our growth into unitive consciousness is smoother when we hear that others too have felt this same pull and survived—whatever action they chose. However we cross over this threshold,[9] whether through small, symbolic choices or more serious and eventful ones, it marks at least one more definable stage in spirituality, our journey into love.

◊ ◊

5. THE SOLITARY REVOLUTION

———— ◊ ————

Verily it is this noble eight-fold way [to enlightenment]: Right view, right aim, right speech, right action, right living, right effort, right mindfulness, right concentration.

Buddha's First Sermon

When still young and in the incipient stages of spiritual development, we must guard against anyone who, in the guise of love, would dominate us away from our highest, perhaps plainest, life. A nineteen year old's comments suggest why objective watchfulness is necessary:

> I'm one of many children. Since last year, I've not set foot in my parents' home. I feel sad, misunderstood and ignored. In their words, I "lack the discipline to work a responsible job." I've always been told that I'm irresponsible, but know I have enormous artistic talent.
>
> My mind is so complex, really beautiful—I don't see things the way others do. Sometimes I wonder if I'm seriously ill, lacking in some important quality that makes people able to settle down. This confuses me: to feel exceptionally gifted, yet be told I'm irresponsible creates my doubt and self-loathing.

No one leaves home and hearth without good reason. If we do depart, usually it is to assert some instinctual, self-protective need, or to express life in the face of lifeless treatment. Many family members would, if permitted, discourage our independence and integrity; their own impoverished psyches are at fault, for the most part, not their intentional evil. Whatever the cause, if we capitulate or make our family and friends our gods, we lose our valuable creative power. In the end, of course, we do grow tolerant of others and more demanding of ourselves. But this stance, if adopted prematurely, puts cart before horse and can perpetuate toxic, stale relationships and a deathly existence.

Each of us must learn when and how to make a clean, surgical cut between ourselves and those who try to wrest us away from life. Part of this work involves owning our choices, taking responsibility and accepting the consequences of our acts.

The film *Not Without My Daughter* dramatically portrays one brave mother's mature decision to flee inhuman, deadly bondage. Taking her small child with her, this courageous and responsible parent was ready to accept the downside of her choice (i.e. death). Embracing that eventuality, all the rest was easy. Inordinate guilt about such separation is largely learned, neurotic guilt. We sustain a much deeper wound when we fail to live out our life as we know we should.

If we trusted our basic instincts (and our power) to protest when our survival and mental health depend on it, we would live guilt-free. Even children understand that there is no earthly reason to accept guilt when, smelling a rat, they try to avoid its bite. The mass notion that equates honoring one's parents or spouses with slavish, non-discerning submission to their every unwholesome whim or predilection is nonsense, even dangerous. (Parent-murders by children who can suffer no more physical or emotional torment is but one example of the hazards in such erroneous thinking.)

Surely we dishonor our loved ones when our passivity reinforces their misbehaviors toward us. Surely we honor them only as we dignify our life and theirs. It may take a lifetime to teach others whom we love how to treat us. Even so we may not succeed. But we can behave as if we respect life and by so doing opt for a fully human existence.

Children as Holy Sojourners

Children rarely hear talk like this. Many assume spirit-draining guilt for what is not their sinful choices but actually their holy, life-affirming ones. If adults had the proper training (e.g. verbal sensitivities, role models), no child would feel unnecessarily guilty. Dr. Alice Miller's comment on this issue reveals the serious damage done when we try to be "good children":

A child . . . can never grasp the fact that the same mother who cooks so well, is so concerned about his cough and helps so kindly with his homework, in some circumstances has no more feeling than a wall for his hidden inner world . . .

Many people suffer all their lives from this oppressive feeling of guilt, the sense of not having lived up to their parents' expectations. This feeling is stronger than any intellectual in- sight that it is not a child's task or duty to satisfy his parents' narcissistic needs.[1]

In fact, it is the *adult's* moral duty to let go, even, if necessary, to force the child out of its nest in order that talents, gifts and destiny itself are served without feelings of guilt or ingratitude. Each child is a sancti- fied sojourner; we adults are meant to protect and serve children.

The award-winning Italian film *Cinema Paradiso* depicts this duty in heroic proportions in a scene where Alfredo, an old, blind movie- projectionist, tells his beloved surrogate son Toto to leave their small village and never glance back. Alfredo sees enormous promise in the young, gifted film-maker. Afraid that the boy will squander his life on sentiment and displaced loyalties, the old man rails at the younger one:

Life isn't like the movies. Life is much harder. Get out of here. Go back to Rome—you're young and the world is yours. I am old. I don't want to see you anymore. I don't want to hear you talk anymore. I want to hear people talk about you.

This is precisely the mature, sacrificial love that psychoanalyst Erich Fromm says demands self-discipline, the absence of narcissism and the presence of true humility. At its core, this love is beyond human (e.g. parental) love. It is impersonal: willingly severing the potentially oppres- sive ties of personal love. Alfredo's gift to Toto involves inevitable pain and loss. The two—father and son—must release each other. In throw- ing Toto out of his secure environment, Alfredo blesses him, helps him follow the life he was born to have. In leaving, Toto surrenders to life's highest call. Only people who accept this pain understand that, as Mother Teresa has said, "Real love always hurts."

As Toto leaves his town, Alfredo, the only father he's ever known, embraces him one last time and fiercely whispers in the boy's ear:

Don't come back. Don't think of us. Don't look back. . . . Don't write. Don't give in to nostalgia. Forget about us. If you do come back, don't come to see me. I won't let you in my house. Understand?

Because many parents of sensitive, self-actualizing or spiritually pre-cocious children feel intuitively threatened by their children's autonomy (and the predictable separation that service to authentic life entails), they hold their children back. Usually such parents are neither cruel nor evil—just weak.

Mourning for Our Lost Light

Hermann Hesse's autobiographical remarks on his struggle to "strenuously construct" his own light, despite suffocation by possessive parents, open wounds that some try hard to keep closed:

> It is a bitter and horrible moment when we suddenly realize that the current within us wants to pull away from what is dearest to us. Then every thought that rejects the friend and mentor turns on our own heart like a poisoned barb . . . the words "disloyalty" and "ingratitude" sound like catcalls and stigma . . .[2]

If, as in Hesse's example and that of the nineteen year old artist quoted above, we feel guilty for self-protectively choosing life over a static, deathless existence, our spiritual growth necessarily involves mourning.

We must grieve fully for our losses: for parents or spouses incapable of loving us maturely, for the lack of vigorous encouragement for our autonomy. This mourning comes in dribs and drabs as well as in momen-tary gushes of strong feeling. A friend, responding to a remark about the inherent difficulties in success, blurted out emotionally:

> People don't like success. I learned this the hard way. When I was accepted to a prestigious, Ivy League graduate school, my friends couldn't handle it—it was as if my success threat-ened them.

> I don't know. Maybe they were afraid they'd lose me, or that I would somehow pass them by. I only know that my good news gave me "bad" feedback from people I thought loved me.

However we grieve, we can be thankful for our feelings. Such emotions heal, are necessary to spiritual advancement. These soften us and draw us into the human race. Forgiveness is a natural by-product of all inner repair. Although we cannot force this, when we've honestly acknowledged and assimilated our feelings, forgiveness arrives on its own, in the form of understanding, acceptance and true reconciliation. The rare person gracefully accepts the inner call, embraces it as simply part of life's overall mystery and joyfully surrenders to it.

Genuine guilt, on the other hand, is not so easily resolved. This, an aggravated, deeper wound, stems from our realization that we ourselves are traitors to our life, unresponsive to the radical call which is life trying to hit destiny's mark.

Faithfulness to one's own path requires enormous bravery. Had Toto not left his village, had my friend not enrolled in her prestigious graduate school, had that nineteen year old not left home when he did, then all of them would have had to forgive themselves later for being human (and no doubt youngish humans at that). As we feel the full weight of our existential sadness (which comes whether we stay or go), we eventually transcend this sadness. Once we surrender fully to the inevitable sorrow of our human limits, we thoroughly embrace the truth of our experience. This welcome also takes heroism, and is an act of humility as well. Our apology to life cleanses and restores us—and this restoration seems the most solitary revolution of all.

A friend and her husband are Buddhists. They plan to retire soon. Previously (while living conventionally in the mainstream of society) they accommodated all the usual family, corporate and community norms and expectations. Now, in their sixties, they feel free to move beyond these norms. They have learned, as a couple and individually, that a complete surrender of control is required in order to move into the truth of their own discipleship. Says my friend, "It's so scary to live in faith this way, especially when your whole life has been dedicated to being in control of everything." Perhaps they are successful because their surrender is non-spectacular, dignified and so well thought out. Mutually, they have planned for their financial needs and are working together to make their plans come true. It seems helpful at this point to explore some prudent ways of growing spiritually mature.

Discipleship to any savior, master or spiritual ideal always requires practical obedience, but not imprudence or foolishness. Even Christ, when tempted by Satan to jump off a cliff, warned that it was wrong to test God.[3] Our discernment and good judgment on such matters depend on readiness. We will not be able, or willing, to judiciously relinquish our control unless we have something else within—a secure bond to our highest spiritual intelligence. This is cultivated gradually. This bond increases both our right action and foundational centering. By admitting our insufficiencies and flaws, we somehow integrate our primary spiritual process into real-world application. As we extinguish the notion that we must change some essential quality in ourselves in order to be perfect, we enter a bigger, more open mind: we see we are already "perfect" in our livingness, our is-ness; this unconditional self-acceptance paves the way for just the solutions we need. Such prudent obedience deserves a further word.

◊   ◊

6. NOTHING SPECIAL

— ◇ —

When people reach highest perfection,
it is nothing special; it is their normal condition.

Hindu Saying

Moving toward self-acceptance involves sacrifices—some easier than others. If we want more time for ourselves for meditative or adventuresome retreats, we may have to give up living by others' rules and time frames. This is a tough but prudent requirement since most of us live interactive, related lives and need some way of ordering our day. We can think of this choice as the sacrifice of collective opinion. We give up caring too much about what people think of us. Other prudent sacrifices seem obvious and necessary, but none of these need alter our outward appearance. For example:

◇ Sacrifice of custom, vanity, security, guarantees, in favor of identifying and expressing the deepest values of our true, inner life: love, truth, health, beauty, compassion.

◇ Sacrifice of living unconsciously, of not knowing who we are or what is right in favor of bringing the law of our being into existence.

◇ Sacrifice of direct and "safe" routes of accomplishment in favor of those which may be more demanding, risk-laden, ethical, illogical, unpopular.

◇ Sacrifice of our particular risk-avoiding tendencies in favor of reliability, commitment and responsibility in relationships.[1]

A friend who is immersed in a popular metaphysical program corrected me on my calling this "relinquishment," saying, "There is no such thing as sacrifice—we always gain something when and as we give up anything." Indeed, seen from an ever-transcendent perspective this is so. A computer programmer-turned-writer gains a marvelous new profession when he quits his steady job. A woman who wants a baby will (if she arranges her working life to allow this) inherit the experience of a lifetime as a parent. The man or woman who relinquishes fear gains inner peace and real love, and so on.

However, before we get the next thing (e.g. a baby, a new job, inner peace) we will pass through a time and place of vacuum—we let go of the first thing (freedom, time, a secure job, etc.) and move into the unknown. This is letting go of control and, as my Buddhist friend knows, it can indeed be scary. Here is where faith serves us and builds our necessary bridges to what we want. A workable rule-of-thumb is to be what we are—not to pretend we feel courage when we don't, or embark prematurely into regions that have yet to call us.

Whenever we consciously let go of something, we find more of that very thing. And, we find ourselves. First, we know concretely that we must have "possessed it" in the first place, if we had it to give up. Our conscious sacrifice introduces us to what we have, shows us what we are made of. Carl Jung wrote that after letting go of a thing, we always have more of ourselves—we exist above and beyond the habit, thing or quality given up. This understanding, this essential bonding to ourselves helps us grow into distinctive individuals. As we freely give up anything, we gain uniqueness.

Our heightened awareness can cause us to consider leaving a secure job (or other long-standing but deadening commitment) long before we do. At a later date (after leaving) we might feel that departing was one of our best choices. In retrospect, we come to value the job or the commitment for its benefits and realize that now our life has a higher worth because we gave up something significant for it. This is putting matters into their right perspective. We have sold all we had, as it were, for the pearl of greatest price.[2] From our joy over this, life takes on new and precious meaning, returning us to soundness of mind.

In *Life and Holiness*, Thomas Merton reminds us that God seeks us more than we seek him. By quieting down, by accepting ourselves honestly, by simplifying life, by meeting ourselves in our own silence (even if only for selected hours each day, which may at first be all that many of us can manage), by carefully attending inwardly to try to hear what God would have us be and do, we more readily answer certain basic, elemental questions of life, such as, "What is God's will for me?" For many (if not most) answering this question is nearly impossible. Yet once we gain some insight our way is easier. What we want wants us.

Prudent Acceptance of Unpopularity

Canadian philosopher Gregory Vlastos wrote that the religious person is an unattractive individual who does not appeal to others because he is a "window to something beyond."[3] In precisely this way those of us who sense the development of strong creative drives or an elevated moral tone can also become unpopular. Our more worldly friends and colleagues may find our greater authenticity and transparency irritating. If we don't enjoy socializing, if we want to redirect our talk to philosophical topics, we are ponderous or too intense. At the same time, we may find others irritating, may feel greater fulfillment in solitary pursuits rather than in interpersonal ones. Whatever social adjustments we make now, we do best by remembering our lofty purposes and by retaining a sort of adult-like sobriety.

A neighbor of mine needs quiet, meditative time. This runs counter to her husband's need for an active, enthused partner in a new business venture. He complained to me one day,

I wish she took a greater interest in our investments—but, no, she wants to read and daydream all day. I don't get it.

My neighbor's wife knows what she is doing and why; she patiently explains herself to her husband again and again, believing in faith that he will eventually appreciate her other qualities, like kindness and a mild temperament that create a pleasant home for them. In order to secure an otherwise fulfilling marriage, couples like this need to learn to talk to each other about their actual needs and experience. Neither should walk on eggs. Perhaps they can best accomplish this in the presence of a counselor who, in turn, can mediate or suggest creative options that support both matrimony and each individual's personal and spiritual growth. Although such counselors are rare, they are not impossible to find.

By itself, a willingness to give up yesterday's conversations and social stimulations in favor of today's ineffable realities is not necessarily a sign of spiritual growth. Sometimes excessive stress produces the same effect. We withdraw into ourselves because we cannot tolerate any more pressure, noise or stimulation—not because we are so holy.

Assuming we *are* answering spirituality's voice—the call of our inner spirit—any withdrawal still seems odd to almost everyone else. But if we are patient and act responsibly, their problem with us is theirs to handle, not ours.

G.K. Chesterton argued that those with spiritual gifts and insight somehow become an antidote to those toxins the world emits. Either we value or express something that our family, community or era minimizes, ignores or loathes, or we embody, as persons, what no one wants but what everyone requires—like honesty, authenticity or deep, pure joy. We are the salt of the earth, but this means we season and preserve beef—not because we are like it, but because we are very much *unlike* it.[4]

Acceptance of Enriching Upheavals

We change. Love itself pulls us apart, and puts us back together again—perhaps inside-out. At first, we only may notice our estrangement or dis-connectedness from the world at large. We continue to go through all the right motions—see friends socially, talk on the phone, behave politely, dress fashionably, drive the proper car—but soon our loyalties shift. Whereas once we belonged to the world and were its agent, now we belong to God. This is a surprise. Our minds cannot believe this is happening. In one sense it means the death of our intellect's rule over us. In another sense, we are (temporarily) engaged in a process of readiness-building, internally preparing (if also resisting or regressing), equipping ourselves for further revelations, enhancements of awareness and unfoldings of our real self.

This interior revolution can wreak havoc on our lives. Especially in the earliest stages, we feel incomplete. We lack information: the pieces of life no longer fit properly, although we may have spent years engineering them into place. What is wrong with us? Why do we seek something so inexpressibly vague? What are we to be? How are we to live? What is to become of us? Why can't we conform to a more traditional way? How long will this metamorphosis take and what will it mean to live the unitive life?

During this time we may willingly give up former things. But usually we do so indirectly. We take two steps forward and, at times, three steps back. Here is when inner and outer realities appear to pull us in opposite directions. We try to reconfigure our daily lives. We think about what it would mean to put certain key relationships into new, fresh mental frames. Perhaps we try telling friends about our subjective growth. Or, we attempt to express ourselves, candidly, when at work, or even at church. Usually this proves impossible—like trying to pour a "new wine into old wineskins." As scripture teaches, this spoils both the new and the old.[5]

Expressions of Irregular Love

Certain prescribed forms of behavior or artificialities begin to disturb us; we recoil, perhaps even from loved ones or friends. We discourage our own over-commitments or dependencies, and this affects others.

We may be content to love others from a distance when their affections are intrusive, unwholesome or suffocating. We may show, as former nun Bernadette Roberts[6] suggests, a certain coldness or callousness that is, at its core, a true love, but on a wide, less usual or familiar scale. Others rarely understand this. But to be possessed or directed in our thinking by anyone else is now completely out of the question. Spiritually speaking, all this is normal and even essential, as any brief review of the lives of major holy persons or saints (in all religions) reveals. Intensely felt religious sensibilities alter human relationships: some of these deepen, some fall away. As we become authentic and globally compassionate we renounce our "special" dealings with other individuals. Our new love is highly irregular: it disallows favoritism, "covers all transgressions" (even our own), lets us serve just one master.

One painful fact is that in increasing our spiritual sensitivities and our immersion in silence, we also grow broadly accepting of others while possibly limiting personal involvement with them. This is somewhat ironic: we internalize (or cognize) the Being values, and our psyches are influenced by more frequent identity crises (or peak experiences, contemplative drives, etc.) and we enter love's mature dimension. Our loyalties are then defined: we become God's servant and not men's.[7] As we go about our Father's business, we find a sacred, impersonal non-doing. This is the let-it-be or feeling*less* side of ourselves. More than anything, our fidelities are no longer strictly reserved for our intimates. In some way, we belong to everyone, not simply or exclusively to one person.

This is neither automatic, nor as overtly smooth or gracious as it first sounds. Imagine, for instance, a marriage in which one spouse becomes influenced by unitive consciousness while the other does not. Or a family in which a teenager comes of age (as did the nineteen year old mentioned previously) while the mother and father remain rooted in their usual perspectives.

A constellation of values, interests and loyalties are linked to each frame of reference—conventional and spiritual. Ram Dass once wrote that levels of consciousness can be compared to different television channels. Traditional worldviews do not see Absolute Reality. Rather those who perceive in this manner will learn to switch frames and see their relative frequencies, or "stations," as merely part of the Ultimate Show. The analogy is helpful, partly because once we see our drama for the fiction it really is, we expand our perspective, watching it from an observer's stance.[8]

Moreover, as we gain direct experience of our own power and divinity, we sense that others are similarly powerful, responsible and divinely capable. We no longer put ourselves or others into closed boxes or forms. This is when, like Gandhi, we can expand into new social or community roles: business people realize entrepreneurial or moral capabilities; householders yearn for celibacy or want "their own space," rooms of their own, vacations at retreats or monasteries; some single people consciously choose to remain so, others find kindred spiritual partners with whom to build a meaningful life; married people renew their vows or undertake exciting, jointly valued projects.

Long-standing patterns of family abuse are also addressed at this juncture. Paul Brunton neatly frames an aspect of this issue:

> Self-surrender does not mean surrender to someone else's ego, but rather to the overself. Merely giving up one's own will to perform the will of somebody else is personal weakness and not spiritual strength; it is to serve the fault of negative qualities of other persons rather than to serve their spiritual life.[9]

Sri Aurobindo (whom many considered the "single most accomplished yogi of modern India")[10] contrasted mundane human perfection from what he called "Divine integral perfection." Reaching for mundane perfection, we improve our normal life without inordinate interruption. Whether we are householders, good citizens or upstanding community members we can consciously scrutinize our interpersonal and moral conduct as well as our inner processes (e.g. intelligence, ethics, virtues, etc.) and thereby benefit greatly. Our aim is to correct and uplift ourselves and thereby find ways to improve everyone's life. So far so good: outwardly nothing much changes. We are, as it were, merely cleaning up our worldly act (although this is not said to minimize our outcomes).

On the other hand, *Divine integral perfection* transforms us and changes our life. This full self-realization is the vital, supernatural perfection which stimulates a complete *metanoia*, that whole upheaval of perception, mind and heart which begets radical conversion. Altered forever, now we shift from willful attempts to improve daily life to full surrender or renunciation. This outcome arrives only by special grace:

> . . . this divine grace . . . is not simply a mysterious flow or touch [from above] but is the all-pervading act of a divine presence.[11]

Although we may continue living as householders, community members or good citizens, everything we think, say and do is subordinated to one "supreme Divine unity and universal Self." All relationships are subject to and committed to "intimate, divine and immortal values."[12] How erratic and variable this can seem.

The Buddhist ideal describes a similar transmutation of relationship, from the personal to the impersonal. Whatever specific life-patterns we choose, as we emerge into Universal consciousness (or "Essence of Mind"; "Ultimate All") we start relating to others on a wholly new plane of contact. The core of this contact is our lessened self-interest and our growing perception of life's unity. Of this, Christmas Humphreys writes:

> The best link, and that which wears the longest and with most profit to both sides, is the conscious treading of the Path which leads, by a thousand deviations and one right purpose, to supreme Enlightenment.[13]

In other words, we find our own self everywhere. We live to benefit others and sacrifice self-interest for the greater good. This too further depersonalizes our way of interacting with others, while ardor for God or Enlightenment may grow. This entire movement can take decades and is sometimes added reason to keep our own counsel.

We can feel anti-social or lost. In some sense we are. How each elects to interpret his or her new patterns of being and relating depends on each one's thought processes, spiritual heritage and tendencies. The fact that psychological (and even clerical) practitioners often negatively categorize such experiences or place highly sensitive, spiritual people into slots with dysfunctional sounding labels can discourage us. The bright news is this: feeling like an outcast is humbling. Therefore, over time, this too proves extremely useful.

Real interior strength, purity of intention and purpose are required for these initial spiritual impulses. Soon some fundamental goodness takes firm, fruitful hold on us. Although I speak gently of the rigors of this side of spiritual growth, my own incomprehensible experience matches that of those who have walked this narrow, demanding line. *If* our self-governing abilities are high, *if* we have practical good sense and have learned to be appropriate despite the ups and downs of a shifting, widening inner world, all goes well.

I have written elsewhere about my move, some ten years ago, to a remote, rural location. My physical move paralleled what I can only call deepening contemplations or sensory "emptyings." Little by little, the things and activities of former value simply fell away, on their own. These turned into what amounted to "dust"—they mattered very little. Ironically, although I craved silence and time alone, my love for others (e.g. family and friends) deepened—yet not in the usual way with its special intimacies. I could not articulate my feelings and, oddly, was unwilling to give time to others. This was not (and is not) a feeling, a personal love, although I felt an undercurrent of growing compassion (which resulted in my taking certain responsible actions on behalf of others). All attempts to explain what was happening proved pointless. I have since found it most productive to just live life and let people draw their own conclusions.

There is no real growth in spirit without cost, no discipleship or thorough autonomy without small, daily relinquishments and larger self-sacrifices. Moreover this discipleship is specific, has narrow boundaries and makes us choose. It is not just the development of "good feelings," a pretty demeanor or continual outer harmony. For this reason, devotion—another face of love—is expensive. For this love we give our life (as we know it today). This both attracts and repels us. Herein lies our struggle.

◊ ◊

7. IMPERSONAL LOVE'S ORDINARINESS

◇

The unbelieving man, like the lover whose love is unrequited, does not believe he will receive if he asks. He accordingly does not love others, and this in turn becomes the reason why he does not receive.

Toyohiko Kagaula

We intuitively know we do not really love ourselves (or our lives) when separate from God. Here we are like the unbelieving man described above. We remain loveless. Emotional maturity, inner resolve, and not a little grace are needed before we can admit this. There are countless pitfalls along the way, as we turn toward a love-filled life, and one is our own imagination. Thomas Merton wrote of this:

> . . . we forget that our ideal may be imperfect and misleading. Although our ideal is based on objective norms, we may interpret those norms in a very limited manner: we may distort them unconsciously to fit our own [absurd, illusory and demanding] needs and expectations.[1]

Part of our work is to separate the forest from the trees of our own illusions. This is tricky—especially if we psychologize too much or over-intellectualize or make small-talk that trivializes our private, subjective life. Then we focus on irrelevancies and fragments rather than comprehend whole-sightedly. (I have noticed that philosophers, who lack a reverential core, get all tangled up when attempting to discuss spirituality; they use one language—logic—and mental construct to teach about another—love's illogic—and contradict themselves as they go along.)

Simple Companions

Silence coupled with simple, necessary tasks (gardening, washing a floor, cooking, etc.) and some routine physical activity (walks in the

81

fresh air, dancing, yoga, etc.) are excellent companions at this time. These order and organize our life, help balance us, and force us to function in the present. This unadorned functioning takes us into love's domain. Without practical grounding, we risk contracting into ourselves or obsessing about subjective, psychological minutiae. All distractions are avoidances—natural but irresponsible nevertheless, since our mind resolutely stands in the way of our own growth.

For example, a common illusion is to imagine that in realizing God we will be rendered "divine" in some stainless, superhuman or spectacular way. This is, in part, why those who seek special powers miss God's mark. In fact, quite the opposite is true. The more perfect our union, the more fully human we become. This means we accept our various sides, our flaws or unattractive qualities. What else but love could accomplish this?

I once read about an early German saint whose friends were put off to see her devouring chicken stew in her kitchen. She was bending over the kettle, hungrily tearing at the drumsticks, broth and meat dripping down her chin. On hearing their concerns about her seeming impropriety she said, "When I pray, I pray. And when I eat, I eat."

If spirituality has any single benchmark it is naturalness. Another seems the slow but steady erosion of self-consciousness. One person may find she just stops wearing makeup; another associates with simpler, less complicated people. He drops relationships with fussy, status groups or organizations. In this way, whatever we are meant to be unaffectedly emerges. As Gertrude Stein once wrote, "Slowly the history of each one comes out of each one." This is exactly the unashamed nakedness described earlier.

Meister Eckhart knew the state of pristine interiority to be far from all, completely and wholly empty as God himself is empty. Sri Maharishi (who frequently sounds to me a lot like Saint Augustine) taught that there is nothing to do, that we must simply be what we are and that we are never apart from God. In this, we have a Simple Companion. Mirroring our state are other uncomplicated externals.

Gradually and always in our own distinctive way, we start to think, choose and live within a trustworthy interior stillness. We may (or may not) actively live in the world, but this stillness is ever present. The point seems only to be willing to live our truths—even if we are not yet *able* to do so.

Willingness puts us on the right track; things seem to work. We become guileless. We start to know what it means to participate in life from the basis of our most sacred heart. If we are preoccupied, scattered or fragmented (and who is not?) then our inner heart opens and "softens" us. This centering teaches us that, at our core, we are love. It is not so much that we *feel* loving or that we cozy up to people like cats to a warm stove on a cold night but that—without inordinate sentiment—we will to do what seems decent, truthful or compassionate. Our bad habits may or may not all disappear; our important gains are made in love's values.

Uncomplicated Disciplines as Gates to Silence

Some forms of simple meditation—for instance, just quiet, regular sitting—are often sufficient as disciplines. Extreme ascetic practices seem pointless. I know a woman who spends every afternoon sitting alone at her dining room table. In stillness, she enjoys the forest view outside her window. She is one of the calmest people I know and brings her inner harmony into her life. Wherever she goes, she benefits others, validating the oft-repeated notion that we can do no better than to cultivate a high personal presence.

Whatever our purifying discipline it is not meant to magnetize any special experience of lights, inner bells or blissful feelings. We simply want to grow centered and aware, and an uncomplicated practice is one means to manage stress, control our mind, and stabilize ourselves in silence. We should not confuse our experiences with transcendence or Absolute Reality, which, in essence, is the Void—not like the phenomenal world. A raised consciousness helps put things right. Soon we see how our own mortal mind draws us away from each moment, and thus separates us from our best good. We also notice how our ideas warp reality, tempt us with self-doubt, fears or unproductive, fanciful trains of thought which in themselves lead us farther astray. Many people report that a solitary self-discipline shows them their paranoia, their projections and their anxious, self-deluding fantasy life. Sitting in silence, walking briskly in fresh air or working consciously at simple, organizing tasks, we slowly shrink any and all illusions, including the one that says we must always be in control.

Dwelling in silence, we begin to listen inwardly with added discernment. Silence invites our attention to that which exists in, and beyond, itself. Thomas Merton's remark that in silence everything turns to prayer,[2] and Max Picard's idea that in active silence we are recreated by the word that comes out of silence,[3] reinforce an earlier point that we must be emotionally ready (must prepare ourselves) to receive those virtues of spirit that scripture terms "fruits." These qualities are already in us, living as latent, potential seeds. "You were always with me, but I was not with you," says St. Augustine to God. We could do worse than repeat, or meditate on, this line daily.

It seems helpful to find a fit between our current spiritual ideals and the values, or ascetic norms, inherent in our faith or religious heritage. I was raised by open-minded, cosmopolitan parents who had a sophis-ticated orientation to life. There was no emphasis whatsoever in my early life on religious heritage, worship or doctrine. As an adult and certainly on my own, I made a series of conscious choices that developed my religious life. Through study, reading, reflection and active experimenta-tion, I determined that the context in which I held Christ's teachings and example was compatible with my secular and community life. Still, even with this "permission" to actively integrate my faith into everyday life, I experience an unending, increasing need to simplify further, to live yet more quietly, to stimulate a larger love that might have wider, practical application. This has meant tailoring my corporate practice to these ends, scaling down work (e.g. lecture and travel) and patiently waiting to see what happens—or is needed—next.

In order to express more fully the demands of this living love, I've taken certain obvious steps to fuse interior and exterior realities. I limit time in corporations. I work only with publishers who respect my crea-tive process. This has been costly, but the alternative would be worse. I have intuited my way to appropriate solutions, inching along, bit by bit. Finding proper outlets for an increasing flood of "impersonal love" is still a mystery; there seems an unending, unfathomable need to give of one-self while not becoming absorbed in contractive, possessive equivalents.

This has meant my finding concrete outlets and creative expres-sions for this innate but apparently radical call. I discovered that I did not have a language to describe my experience or what I wanted or was doing. Another revelation is that, although there seems nothing more meaningful than to live as close to this unitive core as possible, some-times *talking* about this so private agenda is, for me, counter-productive. This might not be the case for others.

Each answers his or her call to holy adventure in a completely unique way—envisions it personally; has special insights, tones and feelings that are almost impossible to transmit. In this, there can be no prescribed form or protocol. Maslow reminds us how dismissed we feel when doctors, counselors or psychiatrists say, "Your problem is characteristic of people your age," or when we're treated like children and told, "Oh, that's just a phase you're going through." It is true that this book and others like it attempt to describe a process of being (or becoming) by listing traits and the predictable experiential phenomenon of emerging spirituality. However this is done in an attempt—however bumbling—to stress the uniqueness of each individual's journey into selfhood, not to assault or deny full-fledged personhood.

Practical Solutions Come From Spiritual Growth

> On the seventh day I also became sick because I thought too hard. In consequence [we said] it was impossible to be a sage . . . for we do not have the tremendous energy to investigate things . . .
>
> Wang Yang-ming, Confucionist sage

Some people with few material reserves and little formal education move along easily, spiritually speaking. Others, blessed with excellent schooling, affluence and power, cannot budge. As discussed in the last chapter, the latter seem spiritually unready. Practical solutions go hand in hand with spiritual maturity.

I have interviewed adults earning *less* than $5,000 a year who have successfully reconfigured their lives in order to be faithful to their highest inner values and spiritual needs. I also know individuals earning over $250,000 a year who feel unable to relinquish even a fragment of monetary security or social status to achieve a life they say they would prefer. I believe such people have neglected to handle the prerequisites to the spiritual growth they crave: positive self-value and learning resourcefulness. For example, my book, *Living Happily Ever After*, provides extensive details and discussion about this cluster of traits.

Adults who lack such readiness can feel fragmented. They may desire painfully conflicting goals: they want safety, security and comfort but this wish rails against their desire for growth. Until their growth-need becomes stronger than their wish for safety, healthy exploration and experimentation will not be fruitful. One man describes his inner pull this way:

> I cannot be expressive enough when I say that I *truly suffer* emotionally and physically from doing work which I loathe. I stay for only one reason: I can find nothing else that will pay enough to maintain my family in even a modest way.

> I think my problem is a fear of scarcity. I tell myself that if I were financially solid I'd have no hesitancy in doing what I most enjoy. Money has become an obsession with me.

This person's dilemma is based on real-life, exceedingly tangible concerns. If we cannot think of ways to support ourselves and our families, it is certainly right and proper to be self-protective. Most assuredly we are foolish to go against our gut-fears. I have received panicky phone calls from people who forget their own security needs or whose common-sense, good judgment is temporarily on-hold. They are relieved to hear someone tell them to stay put (at least briefly) in the secure, financially solvent life they know.

Until we find workable answers for our desired transitions we should not try to be what we are not. "Figuring out" is a skill. This ability, based on a host of integrated, synergistic sub-skills, does not appear by wishing or by magic. Rather it comes by that very training of mind, heart and will necessary for profound inner liveliness.

Fear is always our sign to pay attention. Sometimes fear reminds us that we need to save more money, pay bills or accumulate experience before moving toward the life we say we want. For instance, critical thinking skill brings us good judgment, without which career or personal transitions are tenuous at best. However, when years and years pass, and we are still unable (not *ready*) to take on that which we truly want to be, do, or have, then our real-life, practical concerns (like lack of money or extensive debt or work failures) may be smoke screens covering up resistance or our lack of readiness for the goal.

By contrast, a gifted artist recently wrote to tell me that he and a group of colleagues felt I should have called my book on right livelihood *Do What You Love, Even If Money Doesn't Follow.* Only autonomous, resourceful, and emotionally secure people think along these lines. In part this reader was joking. But he is "kidding-straight"—his humor is grounded in a truthful perspective. He and his friends *are* living the life they want because they can—because they are prepared for this courageous existence. Another, a computer programmer turned novelist, described how she invented supports for her new vocation:

> Three years ago I quit a steady, secure but stultifying job as a manager in a high-tech company. Before quitting, I made the smaller reach into the enjoyable work of starting a novel. While still employed, I sensed I wanted to write full-time. Friends cautioned me that writers make no money and that I'd best keep my job. My family was frantic—I'm not sure why: I've always been responsible. I quit my full-time job to turn to writing.
>
> I have always trusted myself to leave something after giving it a reasonable opportunity to work out. The point is, I've completed my first novel and have moved onto my next. Money? That's the great part. I founded a small consulting business in my home and I work one week on that, the next on my novel, then back to my consulting. I'm earning less than I could of course, but now I have time for books, for taking walks, for writing. I meditate each morning and live simply. I feel I have the best of all worlds—even if my book never makes the best seller charts.

It may seem odd that a book on spirituality discusses issues like work, child-rearing or finances. But when we have entrenched ourselves too firmly in the world's concerns, our minds register these concerns as urgent needs. We are then ill-equipped to turn our attention and devotion to our own spirituality. Scripture teaches, "Thou shalt have no other gods before me." How many of us can name our "gods"? How many practice that one commandment? When we give these secular gods our power, many other "gods" also weigh us down or hold us back: people's opinions, material pursuits and addictions, the expectations of relatives and friends—all these and more stand in our way. We lack answers for life not because outer things or others have so much power over us or are so threatening, but because we are so double-minded. These deficits—thinking, feeling and acting ones—are intertwined. Our own pliability, uncertainty and lack of resolve make us choose those goals (and associates) that counter our highest good. This grand, perhaps unconscious, set-up is one which we engineer so as to drastically dilute our own potential for good, for our joy. Deepening our understanding of our interior life, we build a foundation from which fruitful right action comes. Prayer, silence, associations with wholesome friends or relatives—all these have powerful, concrete consequences.

Autonomy: Another Practical Key

Autonomy—independent thought and action—is critical to the psychological maturity on which spiritual growth depends. Society pays a steep price for our dependency. Dependent people lack creative options, true inner strength to stand on their own two feet or think for themselves, thus robbing society of human skills and talents. However, we pay a steep price for our autonomy.

Dependency causes us to compromise ourselves significantly. As we develop spiritual wholeness we greet our compromises again and—in order to progress—rectify them. This may mean reexamining many sensitive, even confusing questions. Open-ended probings, like those that follow, when answered in truth, unflinchingly, let us feel our helplessness and human frailty or admit our strengths:

◊ What does God's will mean to me in the context of my current life and obligations?

◊ What personal strengths or talents must I *use* in order to do God's will?

◊ What concrete values and practices must I responsibly *live* in order to be a good Christian, Jew or Buddhist (or a decent human being as I define this)?

◊ What is my distinctive, unique vocational call? Am I able to follow this call? If not, why not? What do I need in order to begin?

◊ How have certain health concerns or problems helped me clarify my life's priorities?

◊ What does it mean for me, practically speaking, to renounce my own will? Is this necessary in every instance?

◇ What does it mean for me to "love my brother" or to love God with all my mind and heart and soul? How has my bid for love held me back thus far or strengthened me?

Independent, tough-mindedness exists in both the psychologically mature and the spiritually whole. For instance, in those heroic examples of persons thought to be saints—or simply "saintly"—we find consistent evidence of courageous behavior. Martin Luther, Mohandas Gandhi, Martin Luther King, Jr., and the tireless Catholic worker Dorothy Day all serve as examples of independence. Their spirituality was grounded in their ability to stand apart, speak their minds and, when necessary, go against the tide of current-day opinion.

Many of our personal social acts reveal how we too are moving away from helpless dependence on unexamined social norms and moving into our own, as persons. With growth, we learn to read and interpret our acts so that we not only see our weaknesses but so that we appreciate whatever is finest in ourselves. In this way we recognize our virtue and give ourselves a proper, thankful mental climate in which to unfold. The adage "success breeds success," hackneyed though it may be, tells us why it is important to notice our positive growth.

Not everyone can contribute to others on a large or glamorous scale. But all of us can compare our spiritual ideals to life's realistic opportunities and then merge helpfulness with tangible, personal progress. We can ask ourselves (as this guide encourages us to do) how we inspire ourselves, how we express our values or goodwill and love in everyday life. As noted, what we *think* are our finest expressions of virtue might surprise us when we compare them to what society (family, work colleagues, community) rewards. If we are totally honest in our answers, we find that what we think is worthwhile differs from our peers' opinions. For most people, the ability to love or be virtuous is found in unspectacular choices and steady responsibilities. Sometimes, by contrast, more grand, overt displays of virtue are rewarded by communities or organizations.

As we make time for substantive self-development, or accomplish much good by service in some community project, our impulses toward spiritual maturity assume a life of their own. How can we know ourselves as decent if our actions do not elevate us in our own eyes or if we do not have proper time to reflect, daydream or spend days in "non-doing"? What we do with our time and attention makes, breaks, or remakes life.

The Path of Fidelity

Living out one's sacred, higher or deepest truths is an integral part of the self-actualizing process. This authentic life rarely happens without profound, often intense, devotion to the particular precepts of one's own consciously chosen faith, moral code or highest standards and values. The world discourages such transformative growth. Jung wrote that when we become a personality (i.e. develop wholeness and our inner voice) we pull away from "the herd." This means we gain a vocation, a calling, in the same sense that the early prophets of the Old Testament or certain saintly people are called. To be one's own, in this way, is a maverick's journey in society's eyes even though the individual may feel he or she is traveling a hero's way.

As we accept our vocation, simultaneously we accept certain logical consequences, not the least of which is that we may feel out of place in conventional society. (This is not a given—rejection is no more automatic than is our rejection of other people.) The two acceptances—of our own calling and its consequences—seem coupled, two sides of a single coin.

Our wholeness benefits others. Just as one person's healing inspires others toward similar recuperations, so our improvements improve others' lives.

As we transcend the boundaries and limits of our particular time, circumstance, or society, people seem to see some quality in us (warmth, trustworthiness, intelligence, or talent) that they know they want and need. T.S. Eliot's lines "Music heard so deeply, that it is not heard at all, but you are the music . . ." reminds us of this. We *become* the value or quality that heals or uplifts others.

Authenticity inconveniences conventional life. Our own traditions can give us the solid footing we need. Although inter-faith texts are included in this book, these are meant to lead us toward—not away from—our traditions. The Koran reminds us that whichever way we turn, "there is the face of God." In this vein, no matter what religious tradition we study, it should ultimately point us back to our interior kingdom of heaven.

Our own traditions can support us when all else fails. Without proper, careful understanding we must not admire others' traditions more than our own. I recently heard that "ecumania" is what happens when we begin to think that everyone else's religion and spirituality is better than our own. I want to avoid this kind of cynicism. If our faith is secure it is deepened, not diminished, by our exposure to other ways of thinking; at the same time, our growth helps us relate globally to many ways of saying one thing. Our thinking becomes unitive, universal.

Giving particular, wholehearted allegiance to a specific set of virtues and values and to a particular faith is one way that we grow into fully human beings who are able to hold to whatever is high and fine in our private hearts. This is what Erik Erikson calls *fidelity*, and fidelity such as this is found only in mature individuals, regardless of age. Fidelity is a sign that we are able to choose freely to serve specific loyalties despite external pulls or cultural directives to the contrary. Such faithfulness is exercised and strengthened only when set amidst changing circumstances, differing opinions and conflicting cues of right and wrong. Rather than weakening faith, talking respectfully about dissimilar viewpoints strengthens faith; it shows us why our own traditions have value and helps us make choices.

As we study, discuss and think about our spiritual growth, as we submit ourselves to honest self-scrutiny, we may find that love becomes our primary, radical call. It is a universal beckoning for all those who would grow whole and seems the common denominator bonding all truly enlightened human beings. Love unites us with strangers and the poor; it saves us from taking ourselves too seriously and forms the nucleus around which wholesome strength is born.

Those who express such regenerative love yearn to lend their lives (and lift their voices) to that timeless, praise-filled chorus that worships the ineffable in whom they sense they reside. Here, too, be assured that each one self-actualizes or sings in his or her own way.

One ailing, thirteenth century sister, Else von Neustadt, lived in a convent for seventy years. A few years before she died, she became so physically disabled that she had to be housed in separate quarters. Here she lived, completely alone and bedridden with little chance for conversation with others. She once told another sister who came to visit that she was "as happy as a human being can be on earth." She said that in her solitude she experienced a divine vision about which "no one can say anything except the one who sees it, and even those who see it cannot speak of it rightly."[4] She then observed that she could no longer remember old friends and could hardly even remember herself.

Her remark instructs us that some of us, as we turn toward the things of God, grow increasingly unable—or unwilling—to speak about our subjective experience. Still we can express our love in the simplest things we say or do. For us, less talk is better.

Others develop a full, rapturous voice that they use tirelessly in devotion. Certainly, the Psalms illustrate this voice, this abundant praise. As another example, Rumi, a fully enlightened, spiritually mature poet and mystic of the thirteenth century, wrote eloquently of the divine. In one of his many poems Rumi reveals his own deep, impersonal and celestial love:

> I tasted everything.
> I found nothing better than you.
> When I dove into the sea,
> I found no pearl like you.
> I opened all the casks,
> I tasted from a thousand jars,
> Yet none but that rebellious wine of yours
> Touched my lips and inspired my heart.[5]

◊   ◊

8. OUR BREAD OF HEAVEN

◇

The Psalms are our Bread of Heaven in the wilderness of our Exodus.

Thomas Merton

A restless, urbane seeker traveled the world looking for God. He yearned for the timeless secrets of enlightenment. After years of searching, he came upon an ancient Sufi master. Desperate, he beseeched the wrinkled, white-haired man for answers:

Master, what do you say of God? I've met the Buddhists, and they impress me as quite chilly, too unemotional. Alas, the Hindus overdo their passions and their techniques. I've conversed with Christian saints; you know how dogmatic they are. Surely you have something better for me.

The Sufi master turned away, responding sadly:

My son, go on your way. Your mind is made up. You are too smart for your own good. God wants us empty, as innocent and open as children. You pride yourself on your shrewd, piercing intellect. I can give you nothing for, dear friend, you already have what you want.[1]

When we want logical guarantees or "right answers," the truth hides. Spiritual rebirth asks us to be absorbed in authentic, holy transformation. Our radical, mindless knowing, not our intellect, builds right relationship with God. This bond arrives by religious intuition, not by erudite debate. Logical thought processes (while stimulating and helpful in some circumstances) are but fleshly devices by which we are "always learning but never coming to knowledge of truth."[2] These separate us from that special vacuum that only God can fill. Thomas Merton termed such cerebration "reclassifying old junk in the attic."[3] If, perchance, we meet a true master, we don't know it. We reduce even special, face-to-face meetings to the familiar—continually shift what we already know into old, familiar groupings of attitudes and knowledge. We see and hear only what is expected. To gain from sacred scriptures or prayer we must allow these vehicles to lead us into recollective union with God and, ultimately, into his sanctifying love. This is an act of faith.

The Psalms: Recollection in God

Each reading session is grounded in the Psalms. These draw us into our own wilderness. At some point we may enter a consciousness of Divinity. This mind is, to us, God's own Bread.

With these specific sacred readings we bring our specific, private inquiry into wakeful, intelligent silence. The Psalms can—if we permit it—imbue our awareness with God's own Silence. Many of these prayers are individual hymns and poems; some are exquisite love songs, full of fundamental purity, grace and goodness. It is hard to say where we, as readers, leave off and where God takes over. God himself is in his writings and our proximity to, or distance from, him is what affects our life.

Among other things, the Psalms are meditations of praise and thanksgiving. They are best read worshipfully for their hidden, indirect meanings. The Psalms gradually entrain our thinking, until mind simply recollects itself in God. But we cannot do this if we over-intellectualize or are too literal in our interpretation of these texts. Our aim is not to study these passages as if we were historians.

Origen, one of the earliest Christian thinkers to make an allegorical interpretation of scripture, was certain that the Holy Spirit had hidden God's unfathomable nature in the language of scripture. Just as there are mysterious relations between what is seen and unseen (e.g. between earth and heaven, flesh and soul, body and spirit), these lines of scripture also house visible and invisible elements:

> In the letter, visible to all, it has a body; in the hidden meaning inherent in it, it has a soul; and it has a spirit in the element of heaven of which it offers an image. . . . The invisible, inscrutable mystery that it contains is divine, while its body, the fact

that in its garb of the written word it is a subject of sense-perception, makes it human.[4]

The Psalms renew us, are a means or a vehicle by which, in faith, we deepen our relationship to God and thereby invigorate ourselves. It is this connection only—not what we do on our own, our self-perfecting tricks or gambits—that brings us to life. For example, some people find that if they meditate on just one or two lines of scripture during the day, their behavior or attitudes are improved, without other conscious effort or self-conscious, prideful feelings.

The closer our union with God, the more we naturally reclaim our good, arrive at our particular truths and destinies. Objectively, we notice the strategic, idiosyncratic way that we retard ourselves (or, conversely, advance toward wholeness). Of course, this takes time and depends on the strength and seriousness with which we make our inquiries.

Because spiritual growth is gradual, when we do find answers it is likely we'll have grown better able to use these solutions productively in our normal life. This is how we align our own and God's will. We turn our spiritual awareness (with its inherent, natural wisdom) into practical right action because we have immersed ourselves in his divine, life-giving Presence. The investment of our best rational thinking, creative intuition, and good will in an otherwise ordinary life is an exciting, living dynamic of this entire discovery process.

Whatever personal concerns we may have, we slowly find that we can fold these into a recollective demonstration. We actualize the biblical injunction to lighten our burden, first by casting all our problems into God's "everlasting arms" (which is our primary act of faith). Then, as we are able, we grow into new levels of conscious expression and choice-making. This seems exactly what the psalmists did and one reason why the Psalms are still used today for devotional meditation. One person, growing spiritually said,

I've learned to trust my inner resources. Now, as a result of putting my study to use over two or three years, I feel joy, hope and a willingness to work patiently through all that old "stuff."

I'm ready to go forth, one step at a time, with what I *can* do.

If we approach this reading as something we *should* do to improve ourselves, we regress. If, on the other hand, we read and study because we want and love to, then we release ourselves to that potential fusion by which our awareness becomes saturated with and in God's word and will and Holy Spirit. God's loveliness is the point of all this study, not our emerging purity of heart.

The Psalms: Silence and Sacred Texts

Silence seems *the* profound medium for spiritual growth. Living things develop largely without noise and invisibly. Although silence is especially relevant for spiritual insight, to people who lack either emotional stability or inner balance, the attempt to entrain their minds in silence and immerse themselves in God's presence may be suicidal. I do not recommend it. Silence is a multiplier as well as an integrator. When we are resentful or distracted with ideas of sickness or loss, silence can make matters worse. Talking to a trusted, able counselor can bring relief and break habits of magnifying fears or regrets in silence.

To touch the higher, finer part of ourselves, we first quiet down— much as we do when making a rational decision. We still our thinking, calm our breathing and become objective to our emotions. The sessions suggest one approach. There are many others.

Our active, interpersonal or social existence is enriched as we spend regular periods of time in reverential silence. Some individuals sit still each morning and afternoon for thirty minutes or so. They may begin by quieting their breath, appreciating nature or considering a few lines of scripture or inspirational verse. The many couples who pray or meditate together or attend weekend retreats strengthen their union as no romantic interlude or expensive gift can.

St. John of the Cross suggested that if we would know God we must first silence both our tongue and our desires. Max Picard's idea that silence and pure being go together may explain why inventors, scholars, artists and naturalists all value silence for their creative discoveries and their personal renewal. John Muir (an uncommonly holy man in his own right) wrote that he wished he could spend all his time in an idle manner, "literally gaping with all the mouths of soul and body, demanding nothing, fearing nothing, but . . . hoping and enjoying tremendously."[5] Children spontaneously stop their play to gaze up at the night sky. Instinctively, wordlessly, they are deepened, opened-up in some way by sky's unfathomable, dynamic quiet. Without being told, they sense an imponderable void is both within and without.

Prayers, chanting of inspirational words or sacred texts; metaphorical and practical acts of courage; truth, beauty or thanksgiving; celebratory songs, poems, art and dance; rites of passage; sacrifices and austerities—all these have enabled people throughout time and the world to bond their minds to whatever is, to them, Transcendent. Through these acts and experiences human beings have engaged themselves, as Martin Buber put it, in a relationship of trust so intense that their entire being was one with One in whom they put their faith.[6] Is our era, and are we, so different?

The Psalms: A Radical Call to Distinctiveness

The Psalms serve as a foundation for both Jewish and Christian liturgy and are "the most significant religious poems ever written."[7] Whether we believe that these scriptures mark the "voice of the Mystical Body of Christ"[8] or prefer to identify ourselves with the psalmist David (and by so doing immerse ourselves in his God-consciousness), or simply want to read these lines as religious meditations or symbolic utterances of our own first feelings of self-transcendence is a personal choice.

Surely God speaks to each heart in a distinctive, private way. If this weren't so, why were we created as unique and private beings? And why would he say, "I stand at the door and knock"? Each must learn to listen discerningly in order to open his or her own, interior door.

This, in fact, is precisely how we develop spiritual health. First, we identify ourselves with God. Next, gradually, we assimilate his nature into our own creaturely realities, by our attention and our choices. Then, ultimately, we merge with and into Being, enter the Void, what Buddhists call Nirvana, or emptiness or bliss. When identification and integration deepen, we thereby cross over those fine, unseen lines, from death to Life, from darkness and despair into Light and peace, from our separateness into God's own sacred heart.

There are, no doubt, many views on just what this integration means. For some, like a priest who kindly corresponded with me, St. Bernard's teaching is the rule: Our spirit becomes "unus spiritus," one spirit with God, whose unity, by grace, develops our personal distinctiveness rather than suppressing or annihilating it. Others, a yogi, for example, may feel that this union lets him get in touch with his own spiritual potential. Someone else anticipates boundless joy or feelings of kinship with all living beings.

Whatever we experience, each of us must decide what such union means. Whatever our interpretation, such union is a sort of base line or minimum threshold over which the spiritually mature must cross. Unless this integration occurs, we do not reach full stature as completed human beings.

Especially for those whose life lacks identification and linkages to God, old age must really be a harsh, cold season of "accidi"—that feeling that we have not done with life all that we knew we could have done. Only through our compassionate love do we express the values and virtues of our universal self. This love surfaces itself in diverse forms—community ties; personal relationships; care of animals or plants; passionate interest in hobbies, service, work or family, etc. Only through compassionate love (agape) do we realize the kingdom of heaven within. His Holiness, the Dalai Lama, has said that the essence of all religion "is love, compassion, and tolerance. . . . The clear proof of [our] love of God is if [we] genuinely show love to fellow human beings."[9]

This love is both an inner state and an outer, external response or reflex. We are in a state of love and evidence this in our behaviors. Of course, the deeper and more full our realization of God, the better. Thus, before we call ourselves mature or "grown up," we had best consider the degree to which we have reconciled ourselves to God, developed our spiritual intelligence and responsibly given ourselves over to what we know as our life's vocation to live in God's image.

Sacred Texts as Doors into Silence

Prayerful, sacred texts have helped people reconcile their inner state and outer, external responses. The Psalms (the liturgical legacy of the Judeo-Christian world) are called simultaneously "the songs of God in this world," and "the songs of Christ."[10] These religious poems legitimize both Hebraic and Christian spirituality. Other more concrete—and timeless—symbols and artifacts were used by our ancestors to embrace their spirituality. Special colors, gold ropes or statues of worship or bright lights, certain birds, animals and fish have throughout the ages helped people knit supernatural virtues and characteristics into the fabric of their awareness.

Music, dance, poetry, the fairy tale or myth, drums and chanting or pure, natural elements (e.g. water, rivers, lakes) draw us into an awareness of unfathomable interior silence. Thich Nhat Hahn, the remarkable Vietnamese monk, discovered the following poem about a flower, written by a friend of his before his friend's untimely death:

Standing quietly by the fence,
you smile your wondrous smile.
I am speechless, and my senses are filled
by the sounds of your beautiful song,
Beginningless and endless.
I bow deeply to you.[11]

Silence foreshadows and houses that fertile consciousness of Being (the unitive state) within all of us. Progressively, silence calls us into this awareness, until at some point we live in it, or realize that it lives us. Then, like the poet quoted above, each leaf, flower or bud reminds us of that Heart or Reality or Void in which we all have our life and being.

For some people, quiet is pointless. Not talking, not hearing an undercurrent of noise (radio, television or conversation) humming in the background, may be a vacuum into which fear, negativity or random anxiety rushes. After all, what can one "do" without sound? A more important issue is what happens to us in silence. Silence is our perfect replica of inmost poverty. Sacred texts can bring us into this state. Periods of silence regenerate, simplify and organize life, much as short fasts clear out and rest our digestive systems. Sacred texts are doors by which we enter silence. Silence then strengthens our good will, brings peace of mind and creates for many a new life—*nova creatura*—and the texts reinforce these benefits.

The disposition for silence must come from a grace. Grace stirs us up, makes us want rearrangement. We reach out, perhaps randomly, for the ways to live a truthful, less distracted life. Somehow we discover that silence nourishes us, isn't merely "a finger pointing to the moon," as the Zen phrase puts it. It actually embodies qualities of the moon itself.

The early Fathers believed that contemplation was an experience of God, and that silence was one way to cultivate contemplative tendencies. St. Bernard's word on this, that grace begets good will and that "perfect conversion is conversion to the good," underscores this uniting of grace and our choosing to rest in silence for at least short stretches of time.

Silence draws us into our best ways of being. Increasingly we choose boldly, enjoy the difficult, the self-accepting, the disciplined or the letting-go action—not to impress ourselves or anyone else with our piety, not to "perform" ourselves into God's graces, but because these actions enrich us, bring us to life.[12]

Sacred Texts: Divine Identifications

Sacred texts, words and images do more than introduce silence. The dual stimulation of reading sacred words aloud and then silently (reading and reflecting on these) lets our nature meld itself with pure Being. This means that in body and soul, flesh and spirit, mind and heart, we adhere entirely to lovely, eternal qualities of existence. We enter an upside-down state where the values that the world esteems no longer attract us. We are charmed by positive, unseen principalities, and soon relinquish the unattractive aspects of ourselves, others, the world.

Identification transforms us. In the same way that a child adopts its rules of behavior, feelings and worldview from parents, so do we, as adults, take shape from our Parent, or that which we attend to. To achieve God-consciousness, we fall in love so fully with God (i.e. the object of our identification) that, over time, our own being unites with and takes its tone and directives from him and from his universal, holy will. Of course, the same is true if we attach ourselves to the world. Eventually, here, too, we are shaped by what we love, which is to say, illusion, transiency and a sort of harlot's glamor. This must be why so many of us fear death: having invested in death, lovelessness and the decaying facets of society for so long, we realize that we will be eternally bankrupt.

This matter of identification is another reason to choose our spiritual loyalties and religious fidelities carefully and consciously. "As you believe, so be it unto you" is not simply a prudent saying but an eternal truth. It is with our hearts we believe,[13] and this requires sincere attachments.

We must never force our identifications, since force and effort are the world's processes, fraught with fear, pressure and spirit-draining comparisons. When we try too hard to achieve something, then we measure ourselves against others or then compete to get our portion, if only with ourselves. Then, too, we may drain our vitality through harsh practices before we're ready or use aggressive self-denying methods to try to fit into our (usually) idealized vision of saintliness. If we try to follow some-

one else's call, we deceive ourselves. All this is unnatural. By being artificial or untrue to ourselves, we cancel out whatever innate spiritual
virtues, sensibilities or gifts we do have.

The more organic, gentle way depends on the law of attraction.
This simply means we move cautiously and authentically through the
predictable stages of personal integration, toward what we intuit is God
or our own highest, universal self. Doing this we adhere to what already
is fine and high within. If we are true to ourselves, then we honor our
own intrinsic realities *and* the sacred, timeless spiritual path.

Some rare individuals are genuinely ascetics. But what is right,
authentic and natural for one person can be restrictively narrow—even
harmful—for another. People are different. Their need for such things as
sleep, food, relationship or exercise varies accordingly. While certain
creaturely tendencies such as sexuality or appetites may change with
spiritual advancement, this is not so for everyone. Sir Thomas More, for
instance, eventually acknowledged as a Christian saint, was hungry for
life. According to Robert Bolt, playwright and biographer, More had an
"adamantine sense of his own self . . . who indeed seized life in a great
variety and almost greedy quantities."[14] The question is not whether an
insatiable appetite for life disallows narrow standards of conduct, but
what virtues are we developing?

In some, sensuality eventually lessens on its own. However, not
everyone was born to live as a cloistered monk. St. Francis de Sales'
advice on asceticism is worth restating: "The soul should trust the body
as its child, correcting it without hurting it." Similarly, Buddhist monks
are taught to avoid extremes:

> Two extremes are to be avoided by the monk: being attached
> to sensual pleasure, which is low, vulgar, worldly, ignoble and
> comes to no good: and indulging in self-mortification, which is
> painful, ignoble and comes to no good. . . .[15]

Although spiritual development is an unfolding, one seamless experience, it is possible to identify stages through which people usually pass,
along the way to self-realization or God-consciousness:

First, consciousness shifts. We grow both socially and self-tran-
scendent; we detach. We ultimately pull away from conventional life in
some unique manner.

Next, we gravitate toward a specific devotional path, choose a master or guru or select one spiritual path over another: Buddhism, Christianity, Judaism, Hinduism, or no-isms. The devotional path allows us to express our growing spirituality—virtues, values and creative love. Religion moves us from human- to God-centeredness. Now religion or doctrine becomes a cup into which we pour ourselves. This shapes us, is the context for life's outcomes. For many, there is overflowing.

Around this juncture, many consciously choose to isolate themselves, if only for a short time. Jesus Christ's forty days and nights in the desert is but one example of this physical withdrawal. Buddha also traveled a solitary path, and the Hindu tradition includes the ashram experience by which disciples and seekers leave their homes and spend lengthy periods meditating with their guru or living a monastic life in protected, remote settings.

The object of all such self-imposed isolation is to find God. We can think of this as our "travel into nothingness," the experience of which is essential for final integration.[16] Finally, we integrate our experience of God into our own way of being. Some would say that we are absorbed into it.

From Sacred Texts to Prayers in Silence

After a lecture when I had touched on the merits of prayer, a woman told me that she had been praying ever since childhood. For years she'd kept what she called a prayer-diary:

> I write out all the things I pray about and date this entry. Then I just wait faithfully for my prayers to be answered. I'm always answered—even when the answer is no. The marvelous thing is that I've developed such trust in this practice that I can't imagine not praying. Prayer is my best friend.

A friend revealed that her morning prayer often precedes scripture reading. One morning, worrying about her somewhat insecure future and wanting a predictable, safe life, she prayed for guidance. Then she opened her Bible at random and happened on Psalm 107:35:

> ... And [in the wilderness] he makes the hungry to dwell that they may prepare a city for habitation and sow the fields, and plant vineyards, which may yield fruits of increase [for others].

She interpreted these lines to mean that she could use her busy, often unsettling life more productively:

> I saw I was meant to live in my own wilderness in a way that helps me and others. The minute I realized that we are to "prepare cities for habituation and sow fields and plant vineyards," I found a way to reframe my personal concerns for safety into a more generous stance.
>
> This understanding has turned my present life around, completely transformed the way I approach problems. I now address my insecurities boldly, to make sure I'm victorious—not just for me, but so that my experience "yields fruits of increase" for others. That's how my prayers are answered—in a big, long-lasting way.

The closer we come to our own secret, mysterious core, the more frequently we receive these "big, long-lasting" answers.

Some others might be uncomfortable with so concrete a prayer method. Perhaps instead they prefer to "see" their prayers. In a gorgeous passage in *The Tao of Symbols*, scholar and poet James N. Powell explores this idea:

> Prayers also abide. And prayers are cows. But understanding this requires the imagination of a nomad four thousand years ago in India. . . . The seers of this tribe of nomads know this and their chore is another kind of milking. In the dark silence of their hearts, they somehow *see* poetic prayers, sacred words swelling like udders and streaming luminous meaning until the heart, deeply absorbed, settles on an inmost brightness.
>
> "To think truly," said Heidegger, "is to confine oneself to a single thought which one day stands still like a star in the world's sky."[17]

To see our prayer, to write it, to think, breathe or dance it, to have our prayer become pure and clear like a "star in the world's sky," is to have that prayer answered and our wish actualized in a way that our usual conceptions of time, space and logical sequences are warped or discarded entirely.

Meditative silence (especially when we meditate on scripture or a line of fine poetry) takes us away from over-reliance on our intellect; it moves mind into heart and toward a timeless wisdom that lives beyond logic or culture. This is a word*less* knowing from which all answers come.

The reading process in A *Way Without Words* does not advocate total silence. Most people, even self-actualizing ones, fare poorly when restricted to complete silence for long periods. However, silent times are interspersed throughout the reading/journal (or discussion) process to still the chatter of our egoistic self-concerns. Even when readers use this book alone (i.e. without a facilitated discussion group) I recommend reading *aloud* all selections marked "oral reading." Moving back and forth between silent and oral reading is an ordering, organizing act. This sets in motion a host of revitalizing habits, not the least of which is the practice of reading at a specific time each day, reading aloud (which is an art), truly listening to and hearing what (and how) we read, instead of skimming mindlessly over our text to get to the easy or interesting parts. When we work with a discussion group, it is personally enriching to prepare for each session by pre-reading the silent and oral selections as if one were working alone. Thus we introduce ourselves to the sound of our own voice, reading.

As noted earlier, although my personal focus is essentially Christian, there is nothing inherently doctrinal in the *structure* I've presented—nothing that prevents either readers or facilitators from finding and emphasizing their own focus.

These readings are designed to help us examine our own spirituality, not to proselytize or convert anyone to one way of thinking. Gradually, perhaps, we will want to follow a more doctrinal path. Perhaps not. The scriptures quoted simply help orchestrate what seems a universal chorus of human voices longing for spiritual completeness in God.

Direct experience suggests that contemplation and deep self-forgetfulness draw us into God, in whom we have our life and being. This magnetic, purifying silence has healing power: it fuses time—brings past, present and future to a single still and perfect point. Here healing (what we call the miracle) is automatic. This stillpoint is love, and only love heals.

Martin Buber's remark that the commotion of human life is primarily closed to the experience of unity makes me add that interior silence remedies all problems of external noise. We gain this through our own good will, by managing our attention and through grace.

The title, "A Way Without Words," is meant to reinforce the idea that the absence of talking enables us, paradoxically, to appreciate John 1:1. It is in deep, unadulterated silence that we best comprehend those mysterious lines: "In the beginning was the Word, and the Word was with God, and the Word was God."

The silence of the Word is unlike mere human silence; it is more than the absence of speech or normal sound. We learn this when, in the depths and unblemished sincerity of our human silence, we fuse with, or melt into, God's all-encompassing silence, which is to say his love. To experience this even once is to know That from which all else comes.

The reading process in Part II uses silence as punctuation, pause or an underscorer for language. Just as a beautiful sculpture, in an otherwise empty room, helps define the space, so language—when accompanied by proper doses of silence—helps us enjoy both words and the quiet, promotes our way to an interior emptiness. Verbal *and* non-verbal richness increase.

The state of pure awareness precedes music, poetry, primitive, childlike intuition and every other thing that comes into being. As we nurture and enhance this opulent way of being (and certainly the absence of constant chatter is a means to this end), we realize the timeless void, the end itself, or, I should say, the beginning within the end.

Discussion: The Other Side of Silence

Discussion in a supportive, respectful climate stimulates personal insight. We hear ourselves and others verbalize feelings, desires, joys, hardships or lonelinesses. A properly run support group can stimulate, encourage and even provide appropriate correction, allowing us to relinquish outworn habits or ideas. Growth becomes natural. But for this to happen, each person somehow needs to abide in and live out his or her highest truths, avoiding an over-intellectual or negative mood.

A young woman recently told me that although she now knows what she *doesn't* want to do in life, she can't quite figure out what she *does* want. She wishes for someone to talk to but senses that her friends provide only fearful advice: "They seem anxious about their own lives, so they paint a dour picture for me."

I was well into my forties before I received encouragement for the life and vocation I've chosen for myself. While I'd heard much praise for my worldly accomplishments from friends, business colleagues and family *after* the fact (after some goal or other had been reached), years of work preceding that I spent swimming against the tide of friendly opinion. (I was advised not to work too hard, to take more vacations, and so on.)

Spiritual topics, because of their tender, personal nature, had rarely fit into my social conversations. Thus, the sole encouragement I heard startled me; such full and sincere acceptance for my authentic way (for a direction that I feel compelled to take) was a completely new experience. This encouragement must have been what Buber meant when he advised us to live (or, in this case, speak) in the direction of the other person's life. How many of us give encouragement like this? How many of us receive revitalizing, unconditional acceptance for who we are?

The person who encouraged me did so within the context of a single spiritual counseling session, one which embodied the very elements I describe here. My spiritual director's positive words reinforced a fragile, yet tenacious, inner truth—something I wanted to be and do with my life. My inherent struggle was greatly eased by hearing someone's realistic comprehension of what this would mean. The interweaving of supportive, intellectually honest remarks with my own private truths allowed for release of tension—a sort of sigh-of-relief at being understood. The fact that this came from someone I respected added immeasurable value to my own life. Too many people have told me of their own deprivation along these lines. "The finest human art," the author and dynamic religious activist Toyohiko Kagawa once wrote, "is uplifting others, elevating them to a higher plane than our own." He felt, as I do, that we can do no better for one another than encourage each other's authenticity. This is how we love others as we would love ourselves. By helping people strengthen whatever is already true and fine within, we honor our own love for them and life itself.

◊   ◊

9. THE READING SESSIONS

———————— ◇ ————————

I was in the Spirit on the Lord's day, and I heard behind me a loud voice, like the sound of a trumpet, saying, "Write in a book what you see . . . the things which you have seen, and the things which are, and the things which shall take place. . . ."

Rev 1:10, 19

Each of the seven phases, in each reading session, is a coming-in, a resting-in, or an emerging-from "things that have been seen, things that were, and things that will take place."

The reading process is its own structure. The reading session is meditative, and movement "through" the structure assumes a particular tone, pace and meaning for each reader. In effect, the structure moves us through distinct phases, although eventually these flow together naturally:

Phase I   —Quieting-down.
Phase II   —Opening reading.
Phase III —An oral summary of the main themes of the session.
Phase IV —Journal questions (or group discussion and contribution by individuals) on the main themes of the chapter.
Phase V   —Scriptural readings of psalms (silent *and* oral); journal work.
Phase VI —Interfaith readings (oral); journal or discussion.
Phase VII—Closing journal (or discussion) questions and follow-up considerations for between-session reflection.

As a mindful, respectful approach to the reading sessions becomes a habit, we may find that we introduce a new vitality to the ordinary activities in our lives. Instead of rushing through the events in our day, we begin to respect our relationship with these: structuring, beautifying, quieting or simplifying how we do all things. We remain more firmly in the present. We do things in their own time and in our own unique way. Soon, to paraphrase the *Dhammapada*, we release what has passed, release what is to come and let our mind find its home squarely, objectively, in the moment. Of course, this too happens gradually, without effort or self-consciousness.

Phase I: A Short Quieting-Down Phase

The first phase of five to ten minutes is a centering time. We leave behind our worldly concerns and bring our attention to the theme at hand. This is when a silent rereading of the opening verse is helpful before it is read aloud as an opening formality and focusing device. We establish a peace-filled environment and time our "quieting down" so that the session starts promptly.

Quieting down at the same time each day or week, then beginning to read ten minutes later, builds a rhythm that enhances the entire process so that each reading session becomes a wholistic experience.

We may discover that we want to describe our previous week's experiences in our journal, prior to starting on the themes of the new session. Such reporting of new insights or benefits may evolve on its own; we should simply be sensitive to our own needs. One good spot for journal reports is between the quieting-down phase and the oral reading of the opening verse. In all cases, we use our discretion, since each reader (or group) is different.

Phase II: Opening Reading: Reading Aloud

We structure silent and oral reading into the sessions. Oral reading is rarely practiced. This is unfortunate because human voices have the capacity to bring a richness and depth to words that reading alone can't do. Oral readings may surprise and delight us. If a group gathers around these readings, intending to use the sessions as a discussion tool, the silence and oral readings will add particular value to their experience. For one thing, no two people read aloud in exactly the same way. For another, silence, practiced in the company of others, is an incredibly profound vehicle for spiritual progress. To insure the best possible, responsible outcomes, I recommend that groups locate and work with only trained facilitators for their sessions. A competent, caring facilitator has valuable professional experience in group dynamics. Trained facilitators keep things moving; they make sure that sensitive issues are handled, and generally a facilitator elevates the level of members' understanding of the content as well as the process in question.

Phase III: Oral Summary of Session's Themes

Next, we consider a brief summary of the session's themes. Mentally we summarize main concepts as we understand them from the overview points or from reading *Ordinary People as Monks and Mystics*. This is a short summary, no more than 3–5 minutes. We simply reflect on the session's issues as they relate to our life. An egg-timer can keep our session moving along and honors the predominantly silent flavor of the process as a whole. Much as beginning meditators check the time when they learn to meditate, we monitor ourselves to allow for a natural progression of activities instead of rushing or flip-flopping.

Phase IV: Journal Questions*

Each session lists a few optional journal questions designed to encourage full engagement with the session's topic. However, we can develop our own questions or draw upon our innate wisdom for inner dialogue and understanding. It is important throughout that we members keep a sharp focus so that, by session's end, we feel some gain in productive learning, some impetus to put new ideas to work in daily life in a manner that furthers wholesome and productive inner development.

Phases V & VI: Scripture and Inter-Faith Readings: Variation and Fluidity

After the general journal phase, we return to a silent period to read the suggested scriptural passages. Many optional passages are included if we have time to include these. Then, orally, we read both the additional selections from scripture and the interfaith selections, since the sacred teachings from other cultures are intended to extend the central issues into another round of reflection.** We may want to vary the journal process. Some people prefer to consolidate all their scriptural readings (silent, oral and inter-faith) into one period and then move to journal

---

*Facilitators: Phase IV is a group discussion period, where discussion members share ideas about the session's themes or the opening reading.

**Or discussion, if we work with a facilitated group.

writing. Others elect to spend time in silent and oral scripture: they read one selection first, follow it with a short descriptive passage of those sentences most relevant to their lives, and then continue with the interfaith readings. Here we are invited to create our own tradition, follow or invent our own way. Figure 1 illustrates the overall process within which there will be variations.

Phase VII: Closing Journal and Follow-Up

Each reading session revolves around a theme. The session's main question and title focus us. Then the session details supporting text as well as related questions for journal work (or discussion). This concentration may help us stay with, or address, the main issue rather than drift into side-issues.

During closing portions of each session no doubt each person will want to "sum up" in his or her own way. Some will list things to think about; others will make a to-do or to-read list. One possible summing-up method is practical application: How might we apply, in everyday life, some of the high-minded ideals we have read about in the session? How can we prudently *live* the values we yearn for in our more relaxed, structured or intellectual times?

Reflective activities in the form of questions are provided in each follow-up section. These questions ask us to note each day our responses, choices and attitudes as we relate to a session's dominant theme.

The follow-up questions anticipate several needs: fruitful application of ideals; the merging of ideals and spiritual values with practical, daily responsibilities; the slow, prudent integration of new ideas or habits into normal life; the subtle expansion of self-awareness. *A Way Without Words* is educative: it draws out insight, activity and understanding from our own understanding. Yet because this is largely a silent path, born of heightened awareness—not intellectualizing or discussion—our *application* or living out of discoveries may be furthered by the end-of-session journal questions. Learning involves multiple stages, the first of which is intellectual or cognitive. However in order to integrate knowledge (e.g. insight or understanding) into our daily life, other stages—like emotional understanding—are also important.

When we write out our answers to the follow-up questions, we may want to encourage ourselves to self-discipline: to set aside a specific quiet time every day for reflection, reading or regular journal work. This daily quiet time is an excellent period for thinking about the follow-up questions and meshing one's concrete observations with the information such questions elicit. Despite family, work or other commitments, we try to create uninterrupted time when we can "digest" the readings and pull our personal discoveries into our next day's activities.

By integrating solitude, readings, and meditation into our ordinary schedule, by striving to *live* the precepts of that which lives in our hearts, we help ourselves and others to accept and respect the primary human need for the Holy Spirit in daily life. We also take another step forward into a life that supports our spiritual as well as our materialistic growth. This, it seems to me, is one way to sanctify ordinary life.

Variation should be the norm. Individuals (and study groups) who are willing to let form and structure evolve will achieve greater fluidity and depth of awareness than those who force their process into inflexible rituals. On the other hand, without discipline (like a set or fixed reading, meditation or yoga time) no real progress is made either, since our whims and moods fluctuate and we may not feel like exerting ourselves.

Sequence of Readings and Discussion: A Summary

Figure 1 on page 112 shows us a sequence which seems natural and easy.

Music: Wordless Rituals of Beauty and Order

Integrating music into our reading session can be richly rewarding for everyone. For example, a pre-selected piece of music can be played as we begin to read (or as group members enter the discussion room) and as we finish each session. If we use the same piece for each session, we begin to associate it with the purposes of our reading (e.g. to find answers, truth, etc.) and more readily enter into the mood of each session. If music is used, I recommend an opening selection that induces calmness and sets the stage for reflection. Certain Baroque pieces or children's choir selections are beautifully inspiring at the session's close. Uplifting ending music gives us energy and zest as we put away our reading to rejoin the world.

As an alternative, we can ring a Tibetan bell (or any other type of pure-sounding chime) to open and close our sessions or punctuate a

FIGURE 1

A Way Without Words©
Sequence of Reading and Discussion©

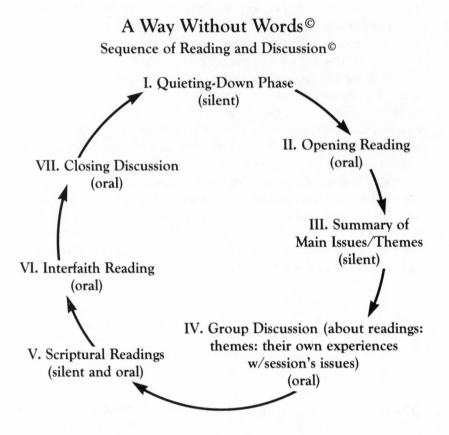

I. Quieting-Down Phase
(silent)

II. Opening Reading
(oral)

VII. Closing Discussion
(oral)

**III. Summary of
Main Issues/Themes**
(silent)

VI. Interfaith Reading
(oral)

V. Scriptural Readings
(silent and oral)

**IV. Group Discussion (about readings:
themes: their own experiences
w/session's issues)**
(oral)

© 1990, *A Way Without Words*, Marsha Sinetar—all rights.

transition into different phases of reading. This is another non-verbal way to lessen our need for distraction (or conversation) and enhance our enjoyment of ritual, mindfulness and order.

For those who like such things, I recommend two incredible pieces of sacred music: *Requiem*, by composer and virtuoso organist Maurice Durefle (1902) and Bach's *Mass in B Minor*. Since purchasing one of the only available renditions of Durefle's *Requiem*, I have listened to it on planes (via my indispensable Walkman), at home—while doing dishes or gardening—while driving. Each time I hear it, I am convinced that this masterpiece is healing to the human spirit. At least it is to mine.

I have a selfish reason for recommending *Requiem*. The best version of Durefle's work is currently out-of-print. It is a Decca Records version, featuring composer David Hickock, the London Philharmonic and the Westminster Boys' Choir. I'm hoping if enough people clamor for it, this rendition will be revived.

My second recommendation, Bach's *Mass in B Minor*, is a lengthier, somewhat heavier, more majestic creation. Nearly two hundred years ago, a famed Swiss music critic and publisher called Bach's *Mass in B Minor*, "the greatest work of music of all ages and of all peoples."*

A client who knows of my love of music shared with me the following story of the healing quality of music. He had read, in personal letters between Swiss psychiatrist Carl Jung and the writer Hermann Hesse, that Bach's *Mass in B Minor* had special power. Hesse apparently believed that Bach's *Mass*, and also his *St. Matthew Passion* and *St. John Passion*, were divinely inspired works, that if one listened to them long enough and frequently enough, one would come to know God. My experience with both of these works tells me this is so.

◊ ◊

---

*Here are the recordings I've purchased:

Maurice Durefle, *Requiem*, Andrew Davis, New Philharmonic Orchestra (Columbia Records). (Note: this is a "2nd best" choice. Apparently there is a French version out too. Don't buy it. It misses the mark.)

J.S. Bach, *Mass in B Minor*, Archive Production, John Eliot Gardiner (West German Records).

Part II

Readings
and
Journal Sessions

*How shall we sing the Lord's song
in a strange land?*
Psalm 137:4

All scripture is inspired by God and profitable for teaching, for reproof, for correction, for training in righteousness; that [the person] of God may be adequate, equipped for every good work.

2 Timothy 3:16

HOW FULLY DO YOU LIVE
YOUR CHERISHED VALUES?

◇

SESSION 1*

Quieting-Down Period   *Phase I*

As you ready yourself for this session, consider your present disposition, your posture or your body's attitude. Let your attention move naturally, without effort, to your breathing until consciousness joins breath, becomes breath. Simply inhale and exhale naturally. Do not force or hold your breath—do nothing special. Just pay attention. Follow your breath in this innocent, observing way for a few moments, noticing any tenseness or holding. Let breath travel into these spots. To release tension you may wish to experiment with "breathing into" any part of your body that feels strained. Simply experience your condition without inner judgment or comment.

If you have brought any particular cares or worries into the session you can consciously decide to lay them aside. (You can always pick them up later, after the session.) During this meditative time, some people find (or create) their own, private thought-language: pictures, symbols or words by which they lift their spirits, leave the world's distractions behind, and actively wait for guidance from their more subtle, profound inner energies—their deeper, intuitive core. Settling down, you may want to consider some lines from one of your favorite scriptures, say the Psalms. For example:

> **Psalm 86:11**   Teach me Thy way, O Lord;
> I will walk in Thy truth.

---

*This session corresponds to the introduction and first chapters of *Ordinary People as Monks and Mystics.*

You can also silently read the Opening Reading selection that follows (Phase II) or perhaps think about your experiences relative to the questions listed in Phase III.

Opening Reading
(Oral—Preappointed Reader)

> Still a prey to uncertainty, one day I decided to leave [every-thing]; the next day I gave up my resolution. I advanced one step and immediately relapsed. . . . On the one side the world kept me bound to my post in the chains of covetousness, on the other side the voice of religion cried to me, "Up! Up! Thy life is nearing its end, and thou hast a long journey to make. . . . If thou dost not think now of thy salvation, when wilt thou think of it? If thou dost not break thy chains today, when wilt thou break them?"
>
> Al-Ghazzali[1]

How Fully Do You Live Your Cherished Values?
(Silent)

Ordinary, everyday people can and do become whole. They can and do live in ways that express their highest and most cherished values—values which also happen to be those most prized universally and collectively throughout human history. Their process of growth is usually expensive. There are costly personal sacrifices to be made when answering a radical inner call. One person said,

> I felt as though my life was falling apart—everything I previously held as important or valuable ceased to have meaning. My friends, values and especially the way I lived—daily habits, dress, work, even my diet—changed. This was so hard for me to comprehend.

> I wanted utter simplicity, needed to be truthful, craved silence and the beauty of nature. I also needed my family's approval for this. For years I was pulled between two masters.

◊

Ordinary people can and do inspire others into healthier, more mature choices and behaviors; they accomplish this by what they do and by who they are—as persons—more than by what they say, have or achieve in worldly terms.

◊

Two primary values of self-actualization emerge along with keen spiritual interests: One is *social transcendence;* the other is *self-transcendence.* Social transcendence means emotional independence or non-attachment to societal expectations, norms or influences. The mature socially transcendent person is even detached from (non-attached to) other people when necessary, not in the sense of contracted inwardness or subjective withdrawal, but because of devotion to new interests, vocation or full, relational life. The "monk" is one who becomes detached emotionally from a known, familiar and comfortable way of life in order to embark on an uncharted journey, inner and outer. Such persons reinterpret their basic way of being in the world. This might include revising the way they relate to society—to others, to work, to marriage, to church, or to any other organization or institution. The long-term goal here is to become a supportive, creative contributor to greater good—however this appears in the short run. Who can say which of these multiple, reinterpretive tasks causes the most stress, pain or anxiety? Who knows how long anyone waits before answering his or her call to adventure, to life and thus to God?

◊

The phrase "self-transcendence" means having experienced, or experiencing in daily awareness, the mystical sense described in poetry or religious literature: the ecstatic moment or moment of rapture during which our small, mortal self melts into the present moment; here we move beyond our normal subjective egoistic perception of ourselves into existence as it is—reality of this instance, now. For some, this instance is a one-time happening; for others it is reoccuring. For all who experience this burst of grace, or love, life is changed forever for the better.

As people move toward their own "inner man of the heart" it is usual for them to experience sadness, or loss, given the countless small deaths (or transitions) they undergo. Moving into a thoroughly new dimension, or current, of life means growing into unobstructed freedom, responsibility and conscious choice-making. In adopting this new nature, we release the old.

Possible Journal and/or Discussion Issues   **Phase IV**
for This Session

Whether you work alone in a journal or with a group in a facilitated discussion setting, you may wish to identify your own, related experiences and compare them to the sentiments expressed in the readings of this session's theme.

To help you find and clarify your own experience and extend your application of these truths into your daily life, your journal comments and/or group contributions could include your thoughts about the following:

◊ What is your present level of social- or self-transcendence? With respect to these two values, what do you discern to be coming your way, for your future?

◊ Can you describe some links between your own *spiritual* health (i.e. as described in Part I—maturity, etc.) and your self-actualizing growth (i.e. individuation; integration)?

◊ How might one present-day value actually symbolize a whole other universe of hidden, cherished values? In considering this, one person said,

> I value courtesy when dealing with others. On the surface, one could say I value "polite behavior." Perhaps what I really value is people—as individuals—and therefore want to treat them politely.

◊ Can you locate similarly deeper elements in your most esteemed behaviors? If so, what messages do your values carry about what you truly want and need in life?

◊ How do you describe experiences where you performed an act because you needed to *get* something (e.g. approval, attention, etc.) or needed to patch up or fill a personal deficit? How might that action/choice differ from performing an act out of an abiding sense of wholeness, where you needed nothing from your action? Compare your behaviors when you need to give "impersonal" or compassionate love—agape—and when you need to *get* "personalized" love, feelings of belonging, security, material benefits, etc.

◊ To what extent have you experienced feelings of separation (or rejection) or tangible social, financial or vocational difficulties as a result of your growth of spiritual awareness, and how have you typically dealt with these?

Scriptural Readings   *Phase V*
(Silent)

Psalm 39:

1 I said, "I will guard my ways,
 That I may not sin with my tongue;
 I will guard my mouth as with a muzzle,
 While the wicked are in my presence."

2 I was dumb and silent,
 I refrained even from good;
 And my sorrow grew worse.

3 My heart was hot within me;
 While I was musing the fire burned;
 Then I spoke with my tongue:

4 "Lord, make me to know my end,
 And what is the extent of my days,
 Let me know how transient I am.

5 Behold, Thou hast made my days as handbreadths,
 And my lifetime as nothing in Thy sight,
 Surely every man at his best is a mere breath.

6 Surely every man walks about as a phantom;
 Surely they make an uproar for nothing;
 He amasses riches, and does not know who will gather them.

7 "And now, Lord, for what do I want?
 My hope is in Thee.

8 Deliver me from all my transgressions;
 Make me not the reproach of the foolish.

9 I have become dumb, I do not open my mouth,
 Because it is Thou who hast done it.

10 Remove Thy plague from me;
Because of the opposition of Thy hand, I am perishing.
11 With reproofs Thou dost chasten a man for iniquity;
Thou dost consume as a moth what is precious to him;
Surely every man is a mere breath.
12 "Hear my prayer, O Lord, and give ear to my cry;
Do not be silent at my tears;
For I am a stranger with Thee,
A sojourner like all my fathers.
13 Turn Thy gaze away from me, that I may smile again,
Before I depart and am no more."

(Optional Scriptural Readings) James 3 and 4, all; Hebrews 12, all.

Scriptural Readings
(Oral—Preappointed Reader and Discussion)

Psalm 39:2-4, 7-9.

(Optional) James 3:13-18; James 4:6-7; Hebrews 12:1, 27-29.

Ecumenical/Inter-Faith Ideas   *Phase VI*
(Oral—Preappointed Reader)

From Bernardino de Sahagun—*Tasks of the Wise Man* (Aztec)

The wise man: a light, a torch, a stout torch that does not
smoke . . .
He makes wise the countenances of others; to them he gives a
face [a personality]; he leads them to develop it.
He opens their ears; he enlightens them.
He is the teacher of guides; he shows them their path.
. . . Thanks to him people humanize their will and receive a
strict education.
He comforts the heart, he comforts the people,
he helps, gives remedies, heals everyone.[2]

Closing Discussion and Follow-Up   *Phase VII*

As these readings may indicate, there are many ways to walk in, or
honor, our own light. These range from experiencing, then recalling, self-

transcendence—the ecstatic moment or moment of rapture—to enacting smaller virtues or authenticities, not the least of which is disciplining ourselves in ordinary speech or conversation.

Perhaps we "humanize our will" or learn how to comfort ourselves and others as we strive daily to be an example of wholesomeness and integrity. Maybe (and this depends on our religious point of view) we see this movement as a turning away from sin. Perhaps we simply want to function effectively, stop our complaining or withhold our energetic responsible commitments. Or we could interpret ourselves as undergoing a threefold alteration in awareness and actions, as do the Buddhists. The three Signs of Being, basic to Buddhism, are the acceptance that

◊ All things are *anicca* (ever-changing, flux);

◊ All "things" are *dukkha* (separate from "the loved," therefore incomplete and flawed);

◊ All things are *anatta* (impermanent, "without a separate soul").[3]

These perceptual (or value) shifts have any number of diverse consequences. One is that we begin to notice what has meaning or purpose for us in everyday life. Another is that we start to examine our capabilities to love—to be responsible for others, yet in ways that enhance their independence (as well as our own).

As a possible follow-up activity, note any consistent acts or circumstances that you create (or encounter) that, for you, serve as examples of "walking in your own light."

One person said, "I am aligned with my own light when I accept life's impermanence on all levels, when I stop clinging to people or my prized possessions or stop trying to force outcomes into this or that pre-conceived shape."

Another person said, "I walk in my own light when I express my feelings—wherever I am." A third said, "I live in my own light when—instead of automatically reacting in a habitual way (like procrastinating, or showing my impatience)—I initiate productive actions: I do what I'd usually avoid. I check my tendency to talk so much. I stop rushing others with my impatient gestures, sighs and expressions. I curtail my tendency to manipulate others into complimenting me."

◊

Between this and your next readings, notice the times when—in your opinion—you live virtuously and authentically. When do you choose in favor of your true worldview (or perceptions and feelings)? Are there certain predictable occasions when you possess increased willingness (or strength) to walk in your own light?

Does your week have specific cycles (say on Saturday or Sunday) when you have more unstructured time? Do you then call forth your self-discipline, decency or light? When have you spent time with special friends or given yourself an opportunity to read something inspiring? When do you accept life's flux and when do you fight it? Consider this broad issue by becoming conscious of your thinking, your speech, your values and your subsequent daily choices.

Learn the art of this gentle, non-judgmental and quite gradual way. Such mindfulness blends both intellect and heart, is simply growth in awareness. This is a way without words.

◊ ◊

WHO GAINS WHOLENESS?

$$\diamondsuit$$

SESSION 2*

Quieting-Down Period   *Phase I*

As you ready yourself for this session, consider your present disposition, your posture or your body's attitude. Let your attention move naturally, without effort, to your breathing until consciousness joins breath, becomes breath. Simply inhale and exhale naturally. Do not force or hold your breath—do nothing special. Just pay attention. Follow your breath in this innocent, observing way for a few moments, noticing any tenseness or holding. Let breath travel into these spots. To release tension you may wish to experiment with "breathing into" any part of your body that feels strained. Simply experience your condition without inner judgment or comment.

If you have brought any particular cares or worries into the session you can consciously decide to lay them aside. (You can always pick them up later, after the session.) During this meditative time, some people find (or create) their own, private thought-language: pictures, symbols or words by which they lift their spirits, leave the world's distractions behind, and actively wait for guidance from their more subtle, profound inner energies—their deeper, intuitive core. Settling down, you may want to consider some lines from one of your favorite scriptures, say the Psalms. For example:

Psalm 84:1   How lovely are Thy dwelling places,
O Lord of hosts!

---

*This session corresponds to pages in *Ordinary People as Monks and Mystics* indicated in parentheses in Phase III.

You can also silently read the Opening Reading selection that follows (Phase II) or perhaps think about your experiences relative to the questions listed in Phase III.

Opening Reading   *Phase II*
(Oral—Preappointed Reader)

As for the Way, the Way that can be spoken of is not the constant Way;
As for names, the name that can be named is not the constant name.
The nameless is the beginning of the ten thousand things;
The named is the mother of ten thousand things.

Lao Tzu

Who Gains "Wholeness"?   *Phase III*
(Silent)

Wholeness exists to the extent to which we are conscious of and receptive to our inmost self. This does not mean we clothe ourselves in phony inwardness, but rather that we stay awake, free ourselves from the tyranny of obsessive thinking, reactiveness and self-absorption. Our life's true purpose is wholeness, the integration of all our sub-selves and fragmentation. This advancement is the real occupation of our human existence. (13) People who evolve toward this high state of psychic health yearn for something unnamable, the nameless, constant name. Sometimes they behave foolishly (or so it seems) while trying to figure out what they need or want. The man or woman who is growing toward this "final integration" can also feel anxious, make mistakes, give up things of great material value—all in the search for "the mother of ten thousand things."

◊

Only in those who establish a link between their own integrity and their functioning (e.g. relational life; choices; etc.) do we see expressed the *will* to obey what is known to be good, honest and true. (22) In other words, our life assumes a purer, if not precisely devotional, tone as we find means to honor our spiritual side in practical, daily life. Paul Brunton's comments: "The Christian grace before, the Hebrew thanksgiving before and after meals were prescribed for the same reason that the Muhammedan's brief five-times-a-day prayer was prescribed . . . to bring the remembrance of life's higher purpose into everyday living."[1]

◊

Progressively, individuals who grow psychically healthy find they get pleasure out of choosing healthfully, truthfully or creatively. As just one example, they may give more time to their prayer life as they find themselves needing, not simply to petition God, but to hear his will. Then prayers become watchful listening—a growth in receptivity. This happens naturally as mature spirituality develops. Similarly, adults attend temple, church or synagogue not "for the children's sake" but because this is one more place, or setting, in which to worship and recollect God. Paradoxically, it is also at this precise point and for this reason that many spiritually maturing individuals leave their churches and temples.

◊

Developing our spiritual natures, our outward acts spontaneously take on an elegance or luster of their own. Manipulation ceases; innocence and truthfulness increase. This is not to say that *every* act and choice is attractive, correct or even effective, but that, on balance, we tend toward right, proper and lovely acts. We function. We grow in grace and gracefulness. For one person this means gaining humility. For another it means added boldness or assertion skills. Perhaps only individuals themselves know when they have been blessed by such grace, although a letting-go of effort or some thorough reconciliation accompanies these advances in grace.

◊

While each one's degree of social and self-transcendence differs, and while the degree of severity of personal sacrifices is as varied as the individuals who are growing toward wholeness, there are discernible patterns to "letting go."

All who are called to a self-actualizing vocation find new linkages, or bonds of commonality, with others who are themselves developing in this way. One of the keys to this communion is found in the type of sacrifices being made. We understand (and relate to) others when we see them severing ties that we ourselves must cut. Another key is our subjective sense of becoming "servants": we want to further the greater good; we naturally follow a higher standard of conduct, or turn toward the things of God. Initially it is helpful simply to become *aware* of the way in which our values, choices and everyday decisions sanctify our innermost sensibilities and, in the long run, unite us to others, in compassion or love. This is a critical point: spiritual growth (final, full integration) happens as inner and outer realities fuse—as we curtail dysfunctional introversion or lopsided, excessive extroversion and live a simple realized life, which is to say nothing special.

◊

Possible Journal and/or Discussion Issues   Phase IV for This Session

Whether you work alone, in a journal, or with a group in a facilitated discussion setting, you may want to identify your own related experiences and compare them to the issues presented in this session's theme.

To help you find and clarify your own truths and extend your application of these issues, your journal comments and/or group contributions could include your thoughts about the issues below. At this point, you may begin to weave back and forth, between this and the last session's themes. (Some facilitators/groups may wish to insert a regular time for the previous week's experiences, based on the previous session's discussion and themes. Either here [IV] or between I and II seem likely places for updating each other about interim events and experience.)

◊ Describe examples of daily choices that you make out of personal integrity. Contrast these with responses made as your reaction to pressure, or as your reflexive reaction to job or other stress.

◊ Regarding the topic of sacrifice, what are some ways in which you have made sacrifices in your everyday life? How do you feel about these now—after the deed is done? To remind yourself of your feelings, you may need to compare your daily acts to those of people in the news, for example, or others who have taken unpopular stands. Even small acts are valid: choosing to spend time in a new way, voicing authentic opinions at a meeting, and choosing not to laugh at cruel or vulgar jokes are all relinquishments.

◊ Some people object to the word "sacrifice." If this is so for you, then what are the ways in which you connect yourself to that which seems highest in yourself or the universe?

Scriptural Readings *Phase V*
(Silent)

Psalm 1:

1 How blessed is the man who does not walk in the counsel of
    the wicked,
  Nor stand in the path of sinners,
  Nor sit in the seat of scoffers!
2 But his delight is in the law of the Lord,
  And on His law he meditates day and night.
3 And he will be like a tree firmly planted by streams of water,
  Which yields its fruit in its season,
  And its leaf does not wither;
  And in whatever he does, he prospers.

4 The wicked are not so,
  But they are like chaff which the wind drives away.
5 Therefore the wicked will not stand in the judgment
  Nor sinners in the assembly of the righteous.
6 For the Lord knows the way of the righteous,
  But the way of the wicked will perish.

Psalm 4:

1 Answer me when I call, O God of my righteousness!
  Thou hast relieved me in my distress;
  Be gracious to me and hear my prayer.

2 O sons of men, how long will my honor become a reproach?
  How long will you love what is worthless and aim at deception?
3 But know that the Lord has set apart the godly man for Himself;
  The Lord hears when I call to Him.

4 Tremble, and do not sin;
  Meditate in your heart upon your bed, and be still.

(Optional) 1 Samuel 3, all; Ephesians 4 and 5, all; Romans 8, all.

Scriptural Readings
(Oral—Preappointed Reader and Discussion)

Psalm 1:1–4; Psalm 4:2–3.

(Optional) 1 Samuel 3:1–10; Ephesians 4:1–3, 11–15, 17–19, 22–25; Romans 8:5–10; Romans 8:14–18.

Ecumenical/Inter-Faith Ideas   *Phase VI*
(Oral)

A Traditional Pygmy Hymn on God

In the beginning was God,
        Today is God
        Tomorrow will be God.
Who can make an image of God?
He has no body.

He is as a word
        which comes out of your mouth.
That word! It is no more,
        it is past, and still it lives!
So is God.[2]

Closing Discussion and Follow-Up   *Phase VII*

In this session, we circled the notion of personal integrity as it relates to two key values (social- and self-transcendence) and ultimately to wholeness.

People grow whole as they receive pleasure from choosing healthfully (i.e. in line with their integrity or highest values). This is not a painless, instant route. Each one exchanges weakness for strength in his or her own way in this most personal journey. The sooner we cultivate objectivity and functioning skills, the sooner we learn that meeting the moment appropriately, without fanfare or excessive commentary, is a large part of this path.

One must have tenacity to consider this route. In their translations of the aphorisms of Patanjali, Swami Prabhavananda and Christopher

Isherwood suggest that many factors delay progress toward enlighten-ment. One of these is our individual level of vitality:

(21) Success in yoga comes quickly to those who are intensely energetic.

(22) Success varies according to the means adopted to obtain it—mild, medium or intense.

> ... No one can generalize about the period required—it might,
> in any individual case, extend over months, years or lifetimes.
> All we can say is this—no effort, however small, is wasted, and
> the harder we try, the sooner we shall succeed.[3]

◊

Between this and your next reading session, take note of your edify-ing choices—the times you elect to grow in the direction of whatever is right, true and life-supporting, or how (and when) you are strengthened in some elemental maturing fashion.

Are your finest choices and small acts seen only by you, known only to you? Do you dilute your self-respect and integrity by bragging about these? Do you collapse easily when doing boring or new tasks? Are your virtues and virtuous acts large, showy or obvious? Do you hamper the effectiveness of these broad-gauged acts by discounting your achieve-ments or by letting others (like family or friends) demean or laugh at your sincere efforts? Have you devalued your best choices by idealizing certain ascetic or devotional practices (or some holy persons), thus over-looking your own fundamental purity and goodness? Do you move toward your strengths (and thus away from your fears) at certain times of the day, week or month? In other words, *when* do you reach out boldly and consistently for your good? What, if any, is the message behind your cycles of effectiveness?

Are there concrete ways that you demonstrate your innate wisdom and enhance your life's integrity? Consider keeping track of such obser-vations (in your journal or simply in your mind). Mindfulness of this sort grows over time. Learn the art of blending head and heart. This heedful awareness is best practiced silently, as a way without words.

◊ ◊

WHAT ARE YOUR OWN FIRST STEPS?

◇

SESSION 3*

Quieting-Down Period   Phase I

As you ready yourself for this session, consider your present disposition, your posture or your body's attitude. Let your attention move
naturally, without effort, to your breathing until consciousness joins
breath, becomes breath. Simply inhale and exhale naturally. Do not force
or hold your breath—do nothing special. Just pay attention. Follow your
breath in this innocent, observing way for a few moments, noticing any
tenseness or holding. Let breath travel into these spots. To release tension you may wish to experiment with "breathing into" any part of your
body that feels strained. Simply experience your condition without inner
judgment or comment.

If you have brought any particular cares or worries into the session
you can consciously decide to lay them aside. (You can always pick them
up later, after the session.) During this meditative time, some people find
(or create) their own, private thought-language: pictures, symbols or
words by which they lift their spirits, leave the world's distractions behind, and actively wait for guidance from their more subtle, profound
inner energies—their deeper, intuitive core. Settling down, you may
want to consider some lines from one of your favorite scriptures, say the
Psalms. For example:

> **Psalm 85:7–8**   Show us Thy loving kindness, O Lord,
> And grant us Thy salvation.
> I will hear what God the Lord will say.

---

*This session corresponds to pages in *Ordinary People as Monks and Mystics*
indicated in parentheses in Phase III.

You can also silently read the Opening Reading selection that follows (Phase II) or perhaps think about your experiences relative to the
questions listed in Phase III.

Opening Reading   Phase II
(Oral—Preappointed Reader)

> Humanity i love you
> because you would rather black the boots of
> success than enquire whose soul dangles from his
> watch-chain which could be embarrassing for both
>
> parties and because you
> unflinchingly applaud all
> songs containing the words country home and
> mother . . .
>
>   e.e. cummings[1]

What Are Your Own First Steps?   Phase III
(Silent)

In the silence and solitude of their lives, cloistered monks of all
religions learn to listen to the persistent voice of struggle, discontent and
longing within themselves. They are sensitive critics of their own hypocrisies and, in e.e. cummings' words, "unflinchingly applaud" superficial
sentiment. This full absorption, these heightened attending powers may
be more natural for those with monastic leanings, and impossible to
achieve in the world's distracting environment. The monk's specific
vows of chastity, poverty and obedience also cultivate and strengthen his
deepest inner awareness. (27)

◊

As we take our first concrete steps toward an authentic, whole life,
we must forge our way toward this heightened, inner-listening and lessen
the world's distractions accordingly. This can be (and is) routinely done
in a secular environment. This is not always easy. As e.e. cummings
writes, sometimes the world's perceptual systems over-train us. We may
define success in largely material or too trivial terms. For example, some

people equate their success with popularity or money or status. Others think they're successful if they achieve fame or a job promotion.

◊

Moving toward wholeness means paring away our layers of falsity and hypocrisies. It also means finding—and attending to—the log in our own eye, rather than worrying about the splinter in someone else's eye.

◊

Learning how to love our brothers or sisters does not mean cowering to their abuse. This too—the ability to stand firm—if separately and with loving forebearance—against those who criticize, exploit or torment us is also part of wholeness.

◊

Socially-transcendent individuals, who live in the world, outside of formal clerical settings, have no ready-made daily routine, no monastic peers, no automatic grouping of like-minded others with whom to share their intense, worshipful stance or their ongoing purifications. They transform everyday habits largely as an experiment, a trial-and-error thing. Because they lack concrete blueprints for dedicating and organizing their secular life to the goals and requirements of spiritual emergence, such persons necessarily design or destroy their own ideas, rituals and life structures. This, too, is a necessary layer of doing/undoing work on their path toward self-actualizing. As spiritually emerging adults carve out a way of life that honors their truest purposes, their disciplines and routines fall into place by degrees. (27)

◊

Generally speaking, with social transcendence comes objectivity, the heightening of rational thinking skill. Self-transcendence brings self-dissolution, humility and a grateful heart. Thus the individual begins to gain patience, keen-sighted common sense and the ability to forego violent attempts to stop this or that old habit. Gentleness (in starting this or that new routine) usually accompanies spiritual growth. Moreover, excessive egocentric absorption starts to fall away as the individual gives his or her life over to God. Subjective, over-emoting inversion subsides as the person sees that lines between "inner" and "outer" dissolve. This process could easily take years. Or a lifetime. Because gratefulness grows, because inner peace is amplified, because love is being cultivated, the aggressive, impatient urgency for "perfection" lessens. Soon perfection is felt to be what one is, authenticity or integrity—not the cold obliteration of flaws or one's humanity.

Possible Journal and/or Discussion Issues for This Session   Phase IV

Whether you work alone, in a journal, or with a group in a facilitated discussion setting, you may want to identify your own related experiences and compare them to the issues presented in this session's theme.

To help you find and clarify your own truths and extend your application of these issues, your journal comments and/or group contributions could include your thoughts about the following:

◊ How do you listen inwardly? When do you recognize your authentic, small and silent "inner voice"? How do you distinguish this from your internal babble, the fluctuations of your feeling-world or your illusory misdirections?

◊ Can you cite times in your life where listening-inwardly promoted growth and health? Can you contrast these positive outcomes to times where you followed a hunch or an intuition and missed your mark entirely? One person said: "I acted on an impulse to put on my seat belts while driving a solitary strip of highway. Shortly thereafter a car coming the other direction side-swiped mine. Had I not buckled up, I hate to think of what could have happened."

◊ Can you describe the types of personal disciplines (e.g. prayer; meditation; yoga; running; craft; etc.) that help you listen to, and respect, your true inner core or sustain your faith?

◊ What are some specific ways that you have extended your devotional life to other—non-meditative, non-prayer—times?

◊ Can you think of other concrete, "first steps" that deepen your spiritual and psychic strength? Swami Vivekenanda wrote that if we can learn to curb our selfishness we develop great spiritual power:

> All outgoing energy following from a selfish motive is frittered away; it will not cause power to return to you; but if

selfishness is restrained, it will result in the development of power. This self-control will tend to produce a mighty will, a character which makes a Christ or a Buddha.[2]

One group member said,

> I find it comforting to hear from others some of the conflicting feelings they experienced as they grow more self-actualized. For instance, in OPMM I read about "experiential anarchy," and that describes my state right now.

◊ Can you express how feelings of loss for old values, ways of life, or former friends compare with feeling lost? In your own words, what inner strengths are you developing? How do these compensate for your private struggle?

Scriptural Readings   *Phase V*
(Silent)

Psalm 24:
1   The earth is the Lord's, and all it contains,
    The world, and those who dwell in it.
2   For He has founded it upon the seas,
    And established it upon the rivers.
3   Who may ascend into the hill of the Lord?
    And who may stand in His holy place?
4   He who has clean hands and a pure heart,
    Who has not lifted up his soul to falsehood,
    And has not sworn deceitfully.
5   He shall receive a blessing from the Lord
    And righteousness from the God of his salvation.
6   This is the generation of those who seek Him,
    Who seek Thy face—even Jacob.
8   Who is the King of glory?
    The Lord strong and mighty,
    The Lord mighty in battle.

(Optional) Psalm 143, all; 1 Kings 19, all; 2 Corinthians 5 and 6, all.

Scriptural Readings
(Oral—Preappointed Reader and Discussion)

Psalm 24:3-4, 6-8.

(Optional) Psalm 143:8–10; 1 Kings 19:11–13; 2 Corinthians 5:17–21; 2 Corinthians 6:4–14.

Ecumenical/Inter-Faith Ideas   Phase VI
(Oral)

> From the sage Yajnavalkya in the Brhadaranyaka Upanishad (Vedic & Brahmanic literature):
>
> . . . According as one acts, according as one conducts himself, so does he become. The doer of good becomes good. The doer of evil becomes evil. One becomes virtuous by virtuous action, bad by bad action.
>
> But people say: "A person is made [not of acts but] of desires only." [In reply to this I say:] As is his desire, such is his resolve; and as his resolve, such the action he performs; what action (karma) he performs, that he procures for himself.[3]

Closing Discussion and Follow-Up   Phase VII

As this session suggests, a first step toward spiritual wholeness is learning to listen inwardly, to "hear" or identify our life-enhancing thoughts and feelings or turn our minds worshipfully toward the kingdom within.

Before we can act in the direction of wholeness, we must identify what this means *for us* as particular individuals. Who or what is it in us that listens? And, as Martin Buber puts it, "Who speaks?" Must you always "do" something actively, to find union with God, or are you sometimes given hints, inaudible (or audible) cues, that direct you in this or that way toward your good?

Between this session and the next, pay attention to those times when you fully "listen inwardly." Are there distinct times or circumstances when this occurs naturally for you? One person said,

> Mornings are my most objective times. You know that old saw, "Things will be better in the morning"? Well, that's so for me. When I wake up I've the energy and drive to untangle my thoughts, to keep my mind focused on priorities and separate unhelpful emotions from reality.

Another person found that he listens inwardly best while shaving and showering. A third said,

> After work (during what used to be an awfully boring commute home) is now my best time for unwinding, for getting clear. I turn on my favorite classical music and review the day's happenings.
>
> By the time I'm home I have my next day's directions. My wife can't believe the improvement in me—this is probably because when I walk in the door I'm self-possessed enough to pay attention to her.

When, specifically, do you unwind or tune in to your inner world? Do you normally resist or look forward to prayer, meditation or contemplative walks or sessions? One person said,

> I used to meditate regularly. Now, no matter what method I use, my mind finds its way back to a contemplative mode. This is my no-thought mind—it's me and it's not-me; but words cannot describe it.

◊

Do you have faith in prayer? Are you self-conscious when you pray or meditate? Does intuition lead you into prayer or does prayer strengthen your intuitive gifts? Who, that you admire or respect, prays?

After a pressured day or season what promotes your productive planning and disentangling? What is your favorite method for centering or grounding yourself? In this matter of centering, consider becoming your own expert.

Ask yourself, "What do I need in order to pray, to live in a more grounded way or to be an optimal inward-listener? What do all these words mean to me anyway?" If you do little else, consider perfecting this art of subtle self-observation. Ultimately this heightens awareness, and stimulates spontaneous unfolding. This direction is virtuous and is a way without words.

◊ ◊

WHAT ARE YOUR PRACTICAL CONCERNS?

◊

SESSION 4*

Quieting-Down Period *Phase I*

As you ready yourself for this session, consider your present disposition, your posture or your body's attitude. Let your attention move naturally, without effort, to your breathing until consciousness joins breath, becomes breath. Simply inhale and exhale naturally. Do not force or hold your breath—do nothing special. Just pay attention. Follow your breath in this innocent, observing way for a few moments, noticing any tenseness or holding. Let breath travel into these spots. To release tension you may wish to experiment with "breathing into" any part of your body that feels strained. Simply experience your condition without inner judgment or comment.

If you have brought any particular cares or worries into the session you can consciously decide to lay them aside. (You can always pick them up later, after the session.) During this meditative time, some people find (or create) their own, private thought-language: pictures, symbols or words by which they lift their spirits, leave the world's distractions behind, and actively wait for guidance from their more subtle, profound inner energies—their deeper, intuitive core. Settling down, you may want to consider some lines from one of your favorite scriptures, say the Psalms. For example:

Psalm 26:8 O Lord, I love the habitation of Thy house, and the place where Thy glory dwells . . .

---

*This session corresponds to pages in *Ordinary People as Monks and Mystics* indicated in parentheses in Phase III.

You can also silently read the Opening Reading selection that follows (Phase II) or perhaps think about your experiences relative to the questions listed in Phase III.

Opening Reading   *Phase II*
(Oral—Preappointed Reader)

The Most Valuable Things

After a wonderful sojourn in the wilderness, I walk again along the streets of a city. . . . Hundreds of neatly dressed human beings with pale or painted faces are hurrying in rather orderly lines to and from their places of employment. I, in my faded shirt and well-worn slacks, walk among them. The rubber soles of my soft canvas shoes move noiselessly along beside the clatter of trim, tight shoes with high heels. In the poorer sections I am tolerated. In the wealthier sections some glances seem a bit startled, and some are disdainful. On both sides of us, as we walk, are displayed the things which we can buy if we are willing to stay in the orderly lines, day after day, year after year. Some of the things are more or less useful, many are utter trash—some have a claim to beauty, many are garishly ugly. Thousands of things are displayed—and yet the most valuable things are missing. Freedom is not displayed, nor health, nor happiness, nor peace of mind. To obtain these, my friends, you too may need to escape from the orderly lines and risk being looked upon disdainfully.

Peace Pilgrim[1]

What Are Your Practical Concerns?   *Phase III*
(Silent)

To carve out a unique and personally meaningful life, we eventually need to build high self-esteem: that strong, reliable underpinning of self-trust and self-worth that says, "I can do all things if I really put my mind to it." Or, "With God's good grace, I can surmount these difficulties." With strong, positive self-feelings a person feels, "Even when I don't know exactly what to do in a given situation I know eventually I'll figure out what to do." Each of us comes to such inner confidence differently.

Some, through faith. Others, through life experience. Still others, through a crisis or a good, stable marriage where they love and are loved, perhaps for the first time. We should never overlook the productive power of receiving sheer human encouragement—like that gained from a devoted, selfless parent, teacher, mentor or minister. This too enables us to realize our worth. Many avenues to positive self-value exist, not the least of which is what could be called Operation Bootstrap: We simply get sick and tired of being low all the time, and have a change of mind and heart for the better. At a dismal point in his life, Dr. Masaharu Taniguchi—founder of the Seicho-No-Ie, non-denominational religious movement—was penniless and weak. He tired easily and hadn't strength to pursue his deepest ambitions. One day, as he was just about to give up, an inner voice cried,

> Rise NOW! . . . There can be no other time for you than NOW! You think you must first obtain funds, sufficient time and physical energy before starting your enlightenment movement. . . . [But] your Real-self is eternally divine. . . . Yes, NOW is the time![2]

A positive inner state is extremely practical. It lets us step out of "orderly lines" and risk living an authentic life. As an example, healthy, high self-esteem merely lets us start off firmly and securely toward the improved life we envision for ourselves. However, there are other practical necessities that emerge as considerations when we start thinking about spiritual wholeness. (38)

◊

Time (not necessarily more money) is a highly useful asset that almost all people covet as they develop wholeness. Free, unstructured time in which to do what one intrinsically desires is an essential building block in gaining robust spiritual health. Most people do find ingenious ways to carve out segments of unstructured time; eventually they want full days, weeks or months to use meaningfully. Spiritually emerging persons say they crave time for prayer, silence or walks in nature. "I simply want time to rediscover myself in a classic 'non-doing' fashion," said one individual. Another admitted, "Now I know why the ancients left their homes and families for life in the desert—one is drawn into the wilderness—of nature and of soul—by faithfulness to an uncharted way of life." (38)

◊

As actualization deepens, we know ourselves to be part of an integrated, cosmic system; we strive to function effectively and responsibly as
a part of that whole. This striving may be what sends some adults to
therapy or spiritual guidance. They feel a need to repair long-standing
dysfunctional patterns or family miscommunications before they can
productively move ahead. Said one man at this juncture of his life:

> I knew I was carrying around too much old and heavy emo-
> tional baggage. I decided to talk about it with a counselor—
> wipe the slate clean so that I could get on with my life.

Out of our self-imposed ordeal is born new meaning, a revitalized
way of being and a cluster of aptitudes or skills which then allow us, in
varying degrees, to venture forth as mature, interrelated members of
society. As noted, improved interpersonal or stress-management skills
and more productive work habits are all elements that fall into this
revitalization process.

For some, a revised way of work and community-membership
comes slowly; for others, change is rapid. In all cases as people grow more
responsible, they begin to expect high standards for themselves or create
stern life-demands. One might expect himself to keep promises and
commitments. Perhaps before he was slipshod or fickle in relating to people. Another now gets pleasure when she stays a course on some personal
goal; maybe she knows herself as restless or quits too soon—before she
hits her mark. These more elevated standards surface other considerations. Time, money, energy, health and relational concerns get newly
ordered. We tidy up these as we realize that if we use our life properly, we
possess the internal and external resources to extend our contributive or
caring reach. (48)

Possible Journal and/or Discussion Issues   Phase IV
for This Session

Whether you work alone, in a journal, or with a group in a facilitated discussion setting, you may want to identify your own related
experiences and compare them to the issues presented in this session's
theme.

To help you find and clarify your own truths and extend your application of these issues, your journal comments and/or group contributions could include your thoughts about the following:

◊ What are some practical considerations or requirements in your life at present? Do you want more time or money or a different quality of life, and, if so, to what uses would you put these resources?

◊ Have you ever known anyone whose life was properly and rightly ordered? If so, what was his or her life like?

◊ What would you have to do, specifically and sensibly speaking, to construct your life along the line you now most want? How might you accomplish this and how willing are you to begin?

Scriptural Readings *Phase* V
(Silent)

Psalm 118:
   1 Give thanks to the Lord, for He is good;
      For His lovingkindness is everlasting.
   2 Oh let Israel say,
      "His lovingkindness is everlasting,"
   3 Oh let the house of Aaron say,
      "His lovingkindness is everlasting."
   4 Oh let those who hear the Lord say,
      "His lovingkindness is everlasting."

   5 From my distress I called upon the Lord;
      The Lord answered me and set me in a large place.
   6 The Lord is for me; I will not fear;
      What can man do to me?
   7 The Lord is for me among those who help me;
      Therefore I shall look with satisfaction on those who hate me.
   8 It is better to take refuge in the Lord
      Than to trust in man.
   9 It is better to take refuge in the Lord
      Than to trust in princes.

   10 All nations surrounded me;
       In the name of the Lord I will surely cut them off.

11 They surrounded me, yes, they surrounded me;
In the name of the Lord I will surely cut them off.

12 They surrounded me like bees;
They were extinguished as a fire of thorns;
In the name of the Lord I will surely cut them off.

13 You pushed me violently so that I was falling,
But the Lord helped me.

14 The Lord is my strength and song,
And He has become my salvation.

15 The sound of joyful shouting and salvation is in the tents of the
righteous;
The right hand of the Lord does valiantly.

16 The right hand of the Lord is exalted;
The right hand of the Lord does valiantly.

17 I shall not die, but live,
And tell of the works of the Lord.

18 The Lord has disciplined me severely,
But He has not given me over to death.

19 Open to me the gates of righteousness;
I shall enter through them, I shall give thanks to the Lord.

20 This is the gate of the Lord;
The righteous will enter through it.

21 I shall give thanks to Thee, for Thou hast answered me.
And Thou hast become my salvation.

22 The stone which the builders rejected
Has become the chief corner stone.

23 This is the Lord's doing;
It is marvelous in our eyes.

24 This is the day which the Lord has made;
Let us rejoice and be glad in it.

25 O Lord, do save, we beseech Thee;
O Lord, we beseech Thee, do send prosperity!

26 Blessed is the one who comes in the name of the Lord.
We have blessed you from the house of the Lord.

27 The Lord is God, and He has given us light;
    Bind the festival sacrifice with cords to the horns of the altar.
28 Thou art my God, and I give thanks to Thee;
    Thou art my God, I extol Thee.
29 Give thanks to the Lord, for He is good;
    For His lovingkindness is everlasting.

(Optional) Isaiah 41, all; Isaiah 42, all; 1 Peter 2, all.

Scriptural Readings
(Oral—Preappointed Reader)

Psalm 118:5, 8–9, 17–24.

(Optional) Isaiah 41:10–11, 13; Isaiah 42:8–10, 16–17; 1 Peter 2:1–11.

Ecumenical/Inter-Faith Ideas   Phase VI
(Oral—Preappointed Reader)

Cessation: A short Jain prayer summing up faith.[3]

Ceasing of illfare,
Ceasing of karmic effects,
Death in contemplative trance,
Gaining enlightenment
Let these be mine, friend of
      the whole universe,
Conquer, for I have come for refuge
In your path.

Closing Discussion and Follow-Up   Phase VII

Between now and your next reading session, observe your feelings about some of your current, practical concerns. Are you satisfied with the way you use time and money? Does your relationship with your job, family or friends (and, above all, with yourself) support your spiritual needs and your growth?

If you feel that you need more time for yourself (rather than more money) take note of how you presently spend available time.

◊ What are your most gratifying uses of "free time"?

◊ What time squanderings, i.e. ways of using time that are not partic-ularly *satisfying*—watch your tendency to judge here!—could you eliminate?

◊ How might you gain, find or buy more time?

As they rounded the corner into retirement, one couple chose to spend every possible bit of their spare time meditating. The year prior to retirement they both resolved to wake up two hours earlier than usual (this meant rising at 4 AM) so that they could meditate before work. They trimmed their household expenses, gave away many unwanted items and bought a lot in a lovely, less populated, rural area. Their plan? To gather, conserve and guard their resources—health, time, money and social relationships—so that, in the autumn of their life, they might devote themselves exclusively to doing God's work.

Sometimes these choices are viewed in health or interpersonal terms, not spiritual ones. A young flight attendant and her pilot husband (who each travel a great deal and love their active, stimulating jobs) built a home in a tiny, unhurried hamlet.

> We need the balance of this small town—we both are in and out of airports so much that life in a rural village is a great con-trast. We completely relax when we're at home.

Someone else might describe this decision in the context of their religious needs. A writer in his sixties moved from the country to a city loft-apartment:

> This is a time of life when I need to be near my church. I want to participate daily in morning Mass, and partake of the Eucha-rist. It is time for this in my life. So, I obey my inner man's impulse.

◊

As you think about the movements and seasons of your own life, what workable plans do you *want*—or need—to make for activities, values or devotions you say are important to you?

Consider this last question slowly, over time. "Chew on" other open-ended inquiries, from diverse sources or readings, that inspire your reflection. Heed the art of this quiet, ambling way. This is a non-spectacular way of personal integrity which, ultimately, unites intellect and feeling. It is largely a way without words.

◊ ◊

Facilitators: As a serious consideration—the whole topic of self-esteem can be all-consuming. It may be helpful to preappoint selected members to do some outside reading on this topic and bring in a few salient points about the relationship of self-esteem to wholesome spirituality or a fulfilling life. Or save this subject for a session dedicated only to the theme of self-esteem and spirituality.

HOW IS YOUR STEWARDSHIP
LINKED TO SPIRITUAL MATURITY?

$\Diamond$

SESSION 5*

Quieting-Down Period
Phase I

As you ready yourself for this session, consider your present disposition, your posture or your body's attitude. Let your attention move naturally, without effort, to your breathing until consciousness joins breath, becomes breath. Simply inhale and exhale naturally. Do not force or hold your breath—do nothing special. Just pay attention. Follow your breath in this innocent, observing way for a few moments, noticing any tenseness or holding. Let breath travel into these spots. To release tension you may wish to experiment with "breathing into" any part of your body that feels strained. Simply experience your condition without inner judgment or comment.

If you have brought any particular cares or worries into the session you can consciously decide to lay them aside. (You can always pick them up later, after the session.) During this meditative time, some people find (or create) their own, private thought-language: pictures, symbols or words by which they lift their spirits, leave the world's distractions behind, and actively wait for guidance from their more subtle, profound inner energies—their deeper, intuitive core. Settling down, you may want to consider some lines from one of your favorite scriptures, say the Psalms. For example:

Psalm 73:28   . . . the nearness of God is my good;
I have made the Lord God my refuge. . . .

---

*This session corresponds to pages in *Ordinary People as Monks and Mystics* indicated in parentheses in Phase III.

151

You can also silently read the Opening Reading selection that follows (Phase II) or perhaps think about your experiences relative to the questions listed in Phase III.

Opening Reading   *Phase II*
(Oral—Preappointed Reader)

Meet the World

Existence will remain meaningless for you if you yourself do not penetrate into it with active love and if you do not in this way discover its meaning for yourself. Everything is waiting to be hallowed by you; it is waiting to be disclosed in its meaning and to be realized in it by you. For the sake of this your beginning, God created the world. He has drawn it out of Himself so that you may bring it closer to Him. Meet the world with the fullness of your being and you shall meet Him. That He Himself accepts from your hands what you have to give to the world, is His mercy. If you wish to believe, love!

He who loves brings God and the world together.

Martin Buber[1]

How Is Your Stewardship   *Phase III*
Linked to Spiritual Maturity?
(Silent)

As people build the strength and practical framework to live their own self-validating realities, they become able to give others the gift of themselves. They have a real self to give. In concert, self-actualizing adults voice their desire to be generous with themselves. Often these remarks sound like those of Fritz Perls who remarked, "I don't want to be saved but want to spend myself."

This wish for self-dissolution in the service of talent, values or growth seems grounded in a perspective that sees the other-as-self. Self-actualizing adults have a demonstrated ability to *act* in ways that contribute to the well-being, care and needs of others. I call this tendency *the stewardship pattern.*

Good stewards value responsible, charitable conduct. They look after or properly and kindly care for the interests of the greater good. We see this characteristic or value increase as people grow spiritually whole.

The stewardship pattern exists wherever love exists for others. Whether we are corporate executives, diplomats or office workers, stewardship brings both psychic and material satisfactions as spiritual nature develops. A secretary said,

> I'm proud of myself for being a good secretary. My judgment is trusted. I have confidence that I'm always doing the best job I can do at all times.

> Though my second love is books and I've always wanted to work in a library, I find I'm able to contribute to this love by donating books to the library.

> . . . rewards come from doing a job well: I'm given time off, able to leave work early to take care of personal things. People trust me to do my work and one feels much appreciated. . . .

The stewardship pattern as action (but not as value) may decrease if people get sick, regress or feel in some way threatened. As the secretary's remarks indicate, this impulse also coincides with the experience that duty and pleasure are two sides of a coin. Good stewards enjoy extending themselves, receive fulfillment from giving and from their responsible, generous acts. (58) As another example, parents who function as good stewards enjoy caring for their children. They do not feel put out when youngsters cry or are ill and need special attention. By contrast, those lacking in maturity, balance and love (agape) easily reach their breaking point when children demand attention or unusual care. Business managers, when stewards, remain late at the office without resenting their jobs or their employers. A friend visited his father daily during his long stay in the hospital. He sensed that his father felt physically better when his hair was properly combed and when he was cleanly shaved. The son brought a long extension cord from home and rigged it up in the hospital room so that his father could shave himself each morning.

Such large-heartedness is what most of us wish to demonstrate when we think about ourselves behaving in ideal terms. Maslow predicted that self-actualizing people would search for the ways and strengths to express their highest values in daily life. Many adults now seek outlets for their need to serve others. They find volunteer work, community projects or care-giving (e.g. like Hospice) excellent avenues for this need.

Thus when we speak about good stewardship, we should keep matters on a sensible level and bring these ideas into our everyday acts. Stewardship is not reserved only for those we believe to be full-fledged saints. The stewardship pattern is part of our own life's motif.

◊

The common thread is the sense of underlying unity that such persons feel with others and to the world. Stewardly individuals think, speak and act from a worldview that perceives no real separation between self-and-other. Said one teacher who travels frequently:

> I don't really know a stranger anymore. Even though I'm continually involved in projects with new people, all over the country, I feel as if I've met them before. I haven't, of course, but my comfort around people quickly turns them into friends.

◊

To the extent we are most ourselves—i.e. authentic and fully-integrated—to that extent we find ourselves psychically linked to others and to the cosmos itself. (54) This is not to say we melt into one another, or lose our personal distinctiveness. Quite the reverse—authenticity begets uniqueness. Feeling secure within ourselves, we are well able to tolerate other people's differences while simultaneously expressing our own.

◊

For mature, individuated persons, gifts-of-the-self flow from real generosity and true unselfishness. These are but faces of love. These gifts might be small, simple gestures—baking bread for a neighbor because of a friendly impulse (for "no reason"); anticipating another's need. Or these could increasingly be motivated by deep emotions of compassionate love.

Because strength and courage flow from the wellspring of our own ground-of-being, as Tillich writes, the greater our relation to *being* itself, the more likely we experience personal power and steadfastness. These characteristics escort us into positive stewardly acts. (58)

Possible Journal and/or Discussion Issues   *Phase IV* *for This Session*

Whether you work alone, in a journal, or with a group in a facilitated discussion setting, you may want to identify your own related experiences and compare them to the issues presented in this session's theme.

To help you find and clarify your own truths and extend your application of these issues, your journal comments and/or group contributions could include your thoughts about the following:

◊ In keeping with the interfaith aspects of the group, you may want to think of historical examples of people who, for you, embodied the precepts of stewardship. You could look to your own family or to your cultural background and cite examples of these for the group. An interesting slant to all this might be for you to comment on the ways your own stewardship takes form or enhances your personal development.

◊ One person said, "It is sometimes extremely challenging for me to reconcile myself with people whose way of life is destructive, who hurt themselves and others. I also have trouble relating to those whose views seem radically different than mine. Yet as I reflect on the stewardship principles, I see that these feelings could stem from my having rejected the potential (or the reality) of these characteristics in myself." Considering this viewpoint, have you felt something akin to this? How do you deal with people close to you whose views or behaviors are "radically different" or who are self-destructive? What effect does your response have on your personal development?

◊ What are some steps you can take at this time in your life to develop feelings of connectedness with others? Have you ever done this successfully? How did you accomplish it? Was your ability to relate in a cooperative, generous manner a matter of forcing yourself, an "experiment" or genuine friendliness that sought to reach out and connect?

Scriptural Readings   *Phase V*
(Silent)

Psalm 112:
1   Praise the Lord!
     How blessed is the man who fears the Lord,
     Who greatly delights in His commandments.
2   His descendants will be mighty on earth;
     The generation of the upright will be blessed.
3   Wealth and riches are in his house,
     And his righteousness endures forever.
4   Light arises in the darkness for the upright;
     He is gracious and compassionate and righteous.
5   It is well with the man who is gracious and lends.
     He will maintain his cause in judgment.
6   For he will never be shaken;
     The righteous will be remembered forever.

7   He will not fear evil tidings;
     His heart is steadfast, trusting in the Lord.
8   His heart is upheld, he will not fear,
     Until he looks with satisfaction on his adversaries.
9   He has given freely to the poor;
     His righteousness endures forever;
     His horn will be exalted in honor.
10   The wicked will see it and be vexed;
     He will gnash his teeth and melt away;
     The desire of the wicked will perish.

(Optional) Mark 8, all; Exodus 40, all; 2 Peter 2, all.

Scriptural Readings
(Oral—Preappointed Reader and Discussion)

Mark 8:17, 21, 32, 38; Exodus 4:15–16; 2 Peter 2:3–19.

Ecumenical/Inter-Faith Ideas   *Phase VI*
(Oral)

From the Ciexaus Ceremony (Yamana): Instructions

Do not seek to benefit only yourself, but think of other people also. If you yourself have an abundance, do not say: "The others do not concern me, I need not bother about them!" If you were lucky in hunting, let others share it. Moreover show them the favorable spots where there are many sea lions which can be easily slain. Let others have their share occasionally. If you want to amass everything for yourself, other people will stay away from you and no one will want to be with you. If you should one day fall ill, no one will visit you because, for your part, you did not formerly concern yourselves about others.

Grant other people something also. The Yamana do not like a person who acts selfishly.

No one likes a perverse, obstinate person: everyone speaks scornfully of him and avoids him.[2]

Closing Discussion and Follow-Up   *Phase VII*

Stewardship flows from our sense of unity, or oneness, with others. Underlying this is spiritual maturity—a firm sense of self, a love of and trust in God. As we grow in friendliness toward the world, our desire to be its servant also grows. We enjoy being helpful. We are willing to be the least (or to go last) rather than forcing ourselves ahead of others, into first place. This willingness is a sign that the stewardship pattern is alive in us. Our prudent, responsible care for anything (or anyone) entrusted to us also signals the presence of the stewardship pattern.

Between this reading session and your next one, observe those times when, in your eyes, you act as a good steward. For instance . . .

◊ What sorts of decisions (or actions) do you make for the greater good?

◊ When are you prompted by good will, affection or gratefulness?

◊ When do you feel separate, apart or disunited from those around you and how does this separateness contaminate your stewardly acts?

One physician said, "Sometimes when I'm talking to a patient, I think, 'How can I help myself, make more money, with this prescription or advice or surgery?' Then I know I've slipped back into a self-serving mode."

◊

Consider how your unique and inherent gifts truly might profoundly benefit a wide variety of people. Consider this sole question gently and over time. Consider it especially as you observe yourself interact with family, friends or others at work. Ask yourself, *"How can I best advance others' lives through my talents, my family or community life or my interests?"*

Learn this ongoing, meditative art, a silent self-inquiry. The way of expanded awareness saves energy and pain and is meant to be practiced without judgment, pressure or haste. This way blends mind and heart, eventually producing "no mind." Your "no mind" is healing and flows from this way without words.

◊ ◊

WHAT ARE YOUR "GIFTS OF SELF"?

◇

SESSION 6*

Quieting-Down Period   *Phase I*

As you ready yourself for this session, consider your present disposition, your posture or your body's attitude. Let your attention move naturally, without effort, to your breathing until consciousness joins breath, becomes breath. Simply inhale and exhale naturally. Do not force or hold your breath—do nothing special. Just pay attention. Follow your breath in this innocent, observing way for a few moments, noticing any tenseness or holding. Let breath travel into these spots. To release tension you may wish to experiment with "breathing into" any part of your body that feels strained. Simply experience your condition without inner judgment or comment.

If you have brought any particular cares or worries into the session you can consciously decide to lay them aside. (You can always pick them up later, after the session.) During this meditative time, some people find (or create) their own, private thought-language: pictures, symbols or words by which they lift their spirits, leave the world's distractions behind, and actively wait for guidance from their more subtle, profound inner energies—their deeper, intuitive core. Settling down, you may want to consider some lines from one of your favorite scriptures, say the Psalms. For example:

> **Psalm 55:1–2**   Give ear to my prayer, O God;
> And do not hide Thyself from my supplication.
> Give heed to me, and answer me;
> I am restless in my complaint. . . .

---

*This session corresponds to pages in *Ordinary People as Monks and Mystics* indicated in parentheses in Phase III.

159

You can also silently read the Opening Reading selection that follows (Phase II) or perhaps think about your experiences relative to the questions listed in Phase III.

Opening Reading   *Phase II*
(Oral—Preappointed Reader)

> If one corner of my life is in disorder then the whole of my life is in disorder. So you shouldn't ask how to put one corner in order but why I have broken life into so many different fragments. . . . I should ask myself whether I am going to stay in some sordid little room of pleasure all my life. Go into the slavery of each pleasure, each fragment, and say to yourself, my God, I am dependent, I am a slave to all these little corners—is that all there is in my life? Stay with it and see what happens.
>
> . . . The loneliness, bleakness, wretchedness you feel without [your lover/other-as-love-object] existed before you fell in love. What you call love is merely stimulation, the temporary covering up of your emptiness. You escaped from loneliness through a person, used this person to cover it up. Your problem is not this relationship but rather it is the problem of your own emptiness. Escape is very dangerous, because like some drugs, it hides the real problem. It is because you have no love inside you that you continually look for love from the outside.
>
> Krishnamurti[1]

What Are Your "Gifts of Self"?   *Phase III*
(Silent)

Whatever the form, love's potency and force is always present to some degree in true giving. In giving of ourselves, we give from strength—not from weakness, fear or exploitation. The latter, as motives, show that we are controlled by our deficits, have submitted to external pressures or seek to get something from another through "giving." A gift of the self is evident whenever our offering carries with it something of value from our essential being and sufficiencies. The parent who cares for the child without expecting gratitude or comfort in return surrenders self-interest for the needs of the other. Whether we give a great deal or a small amount matters less than whether we extend ourselves, put ourselves empathically into the shoes of the other or provide something that we intuitively know is needed or wanted. In Luke 21 we read that a widow who gave two small copper coins put into the treasury "more than any [of the rich]," for she gave out of her poverty—not her surplus. (59)

Emotionally tormented by his parents during childhood, one man still helped them financially during their old age. This required his assuming extra jobs and depriving himself of things he wanted—even time with his own loved ones. He explained,

> I looked to what I'd want if I were in their shoes. This solution came to me as a viable, decent one. This is all I'm able to share—not time. Emotions and memory must be put aside. It still hurts too much to visit. My familial affections are strained, perhaps—on a feeling level—lacking. I give out of poverty—which, in my case, means impoverished love.

A woman lived on a tiny pension. She loved the company of friends, especially when they came to her home for dinner. It was her custom to prepare meals with utmost care, stretch the amount of food with potatoes or pasta, and use her guests' house-gifts (e.g. wine, candy, flowers) to augment her simple offering.

This woman gives twice: once when she feeds others in celebration of old friendships and general sociability; next when she graciously uses her friends' presents and helps them become generous givers as well.

◊

Through his parables, Jesus taught that it is not those who are healthy who need doctors, but those who are sick.[2] In this same way, from our sicknesses—i.e. our personal impoverishments—come our most lavish offerings. Usually only we know the cost of such gifts. St. Benedict Labre's comment that to love God we need three hearts—a heart of fire (for God), a fleshy heart (for others) and a bronze heart for ourselves—explains the good steward's interior domain.

◊

The attitudes and actions of good stewards show us a threefold psychology of stewardship. Good stewards, consciously or not, desire a

deeper, fuller identity with their soul, want to plumb the depths of themselves by virtue of all their actions. The second characteristic of stewardship, as noted, is that individuals experience a sense of kinship with
others. In this, their giving almost seems a gift to themselves, an expression of the Golden Rule. Third, good stewards develop a potent, progressively dynamic type of love. As the man's example illustrates, they
"love against" their feelings or their memory. This state enhances their
life in almost every way.

     The good steward's love *is* a giving and a receiving—the individual
exhibits active love through his or her thoughts, works or social activities; thus we say these are "gifts of self." Something from within that person's spirit passes through to others who then either respond in kind or
simply receive the gift. Since the steward *needs* to give, the fact that there
is a ready market for this love is in itself a reward. The old saying, "The
'bad' person gives the 'good' person a job," helps express this point. (60)

Possible Journal and/or Discussion Issues   Phase IV
for This Session

     Whether you are working alone, in a journal, or with a group in a
facilitated discussion setting, you may want to identify your own related
experiences and compare them to the issues presented in this session's
theme.

     To help you find and clarify your own truths and extend your
application of these issues, your journal comments and/or group contributions could include your thoughts about the following:

◊ How do you (or those you know) express your (or their) unique gifts
through work, particularly if a job is outwardly mundane? Would you
say this is a "gift of self"? Why or why not?

◊ Whom do you know (or whom have you read about) who manages
to accomplish this? In your own case, what impoverishments prompt
or feed your stewardly acts?

◊ Even if we aren't doing something that is traditionally viewed as creative, how might we make an art of giving creatively in our daily
lives—for instance, expressing our distinctive self despite tedium?
How does this relate to stewardship and/or cultivating a "potent,

progressively dynamic" love? What personal potencies have you experienced as a good steward?

◊ Do you believe that meaning/meaninglessness is self-created or is it inherent in a particular way of life, or type of work? What keeps you/us from finding meaning in everyday life? Are there times when meaning is present and other times when it's hard to experience? Can you relate good stewardship to added purpose or meaning in life? If so, what does this suggest in terms of your daily actions or goals?

◊ What *small* act might you do next week to demonstrate your investment of love, or your stewardly care, for others? If in a study group, would you be willing to report back to the group if you tried this? (Note: Some group members may already be highly involved in community projects. They may want to simply reinterpret their current activities through the filter of these issues and texts.)

Scriptural Readings   *Phase V*
(Silent)

Psalm 91:
1   He who dwells in the shelter of the Most High
    Will abide in the shadow of the Almighty.
2   I will say to the Lord, "My refuge and my fortress,
    My God, in whom I trust!"
3   For it is He who delivers you from the snare of the trapper,
    And from the deadly pestilence.
4   He will cover you with His pinions,
    And under His wings you may seek refuge;
    His faithfulness is a shield and bulwark.

5   You will not be afraid of the terror by night,
    Or of the arrow that flies by day;
6   Of the pestilence that stalks in darkness,
    Or of the destruction that lays waste at noon.
7   A thousand may fall at your side,
    And ten thousand at your right hand;
    But it shall not approach you.

8 You will only look on with your eyes,
And see the recompense of the wicked.

9 For you have made the Lord your refuge,
Even the Most High, your dwelling place.

10 No evil will befall you,
Nor will any plague come near your tent.

11 For He will give His angels charge concerning you,
To guard you in all your ways.

12 They will bear you up in their hands,
Lest you strike your foot against a stone.

13 You will tread upon the lion and cobra,
The young lion and the serpent you will trample down.

14 "Because he has loved Me, therefore I will deliver him;
I will set him securely on high, because he has known My name.

15 He will call upon Me, and I will answer him;
I will be with him in trouble;
I will rescue him and honor him.

16 With a long life I will satisfy him,
And let him behold My salvation."

(Optional) 1 Corinthians, 1 and 2, all; 1 Chronicles 29, all; Acts 2, all.

Scriptural Readings
(Oral—Preappointed Reader and Discussion)

1 Corinthians 1:25–27; 1 Corinthians 2:12–16;

1 Chronicles 29:9–11; Acts 2:42–47.

Ecumenical/Inter-Faith Ideas   *Phase VI*
(Oral)

From Confucius:

Tzu-kung asked, "Is there one word which can express the essence of right conduct in life?" K'ung replied: "It is the word *shu*—reciprocity: Do not do to others what you do not want them to do to you."[3]

◊

From Sikhism:

He alone is truly truthful
        In whose heart is the True One living,
Whose soul within is rinsed of falsehood
        And his body without is cleansed by washing.

He alone is truly truthful
        Who loves truth with passion,
Whose heart rejoices in the Name. . . .
        And finds the door to salvation.[4] (336)

Closing Discussion and Follow-Up   *Phase VII*

This session quotes Krishnamurti on our tendency to desire (and give) love out of fragmentation or emptiness rather than from strength or true generosity.

Between this and your next reading session, observe those times when you spot the differences between these two ways of being *in your-self*. Please do not spend your time examining others' motives (since no one ever can tell what motivates another person). The constant worry about what others think, feel or intend is simply a distraction—keeping us from taking out the log in our own eye. Consider these issues:

◊ When are you likely to perform acts of love out of "neediness"?

◊ When do you know you are giving a gift-of-self, a generous, non-exploitive, act of love?

◊ What different elements (e.g. people; circumstances; your own comfort with another) are involved in these two times?

◊ Generally speaking, when are you most generous, strong and able to give? (What precedes these strong times?)

◊ Keep your attention on this last question over time. Your answer may help build the large-heartedness that you desire.

◊

Consider such questions gently, non-judgmentally, and over time learn the way of this art. It is clear-minded and ultimately practiced in silence. This brings awareness to a single, still-point of understanding. This is an empty way—a way without words.

◊ ◊

WHAT PART DOES SILENCE
PLAY IN YOUR LIFE?

———————— ◇ ————————

SESSION 7*

Quieting-Down Period   *Phase I*

As you ready yourself for this session, consider your present disposition, your posture or your body's attitude. Let your attention move naturally, without effort, to your breathing until consciousness joins breath, becomes breath. Simply inhale and exhale naturally. Do not force your breath—do nothing special. Just pay attention. Follow your breath in this innocent, observing way for a few moments, noticing any tenseness or holding. Let breath travel into these spots. To release tension you may wish to experiment with "breathing into" any part of your body that feels strained. Simply experience your condition without inner judgment or comment.

If you have brought any particular cares or worries into the session you can consciously decide to lay them aside. (You can always pick them up later, after the session.) During this meditative time, some people find, or create, their own, private thought-language: pictures, symbols or words by which they lift their spirits, leave the world's distractions behind, and actively wait for guidance from their more subtle, profound inner energies—their deeper, intuitive core. Settling down, you may want to consider some lines from one of your favorite scriptures, say the Psalms. For example:

Psalm 10   Hear me, O Lord, and be gracious to me;
              O Lord, be Thou my helper.

————————————

*This session corresponds to pages in *Ordinary People as Monks and Mystics* indicated in parentheses in Phase III.

You can also silently read the Opening Reading selection that follows (Phase II) or consider your experience relative to the questions listed in Phase III.

Opening Reading   *Phase II*
(Oral—Preappointed Reader)

The Greek statues were like vessels of silence. They stood
there in rows, and man passed between them as along an
avenue of silence.

The silence was confined in the statues and became a
splendor over their whiteness.

Their silence is full of mystery. It is as though they remain
silent as long as man stands before them and as if they begin to
speak as soon as they are alone. They speak to the gods, but
they are silent to man.

The marble statues of the Greek gods lie embedded like
white islands of silence in the midst of the noise of the world
today. . . .

The silence that is in the Greek statues does not oppress
them: it is a light and radiant silence. The figure is master over
the silence: at any moment the word can arise from the silence
like a God from Olympus.[1]

What Part Does Silence Play   *Phase III*
in Your Life?
(Silent)

◊ It is in silence that our reflective ability—and our need to reflect—is
born. Silence makes us grow progressively aware: sounds, however
distant—or the absence of them—bring out hidden parts of us.
Silence triggers thoughts or feelings and various fleeting phenomena.
It is in silence that we perceive life's omnipresent, omniscient dimension; in silence we meet the ineffable. Silence (and solitude) affirm
and strengthen our individuality. Phenomenal life loses its grip on our
minds the longer we live in silence—a constant, bright true reality.
(148)

◊ Any number of solitary practices assist in developing wholeness. By solitary practices I mean various formal meditations such as the ancient forms of prayer common to the Judeo-Christian mystical tradition or practices such as the Zen procedure called zazen or classical mantra meditations which may have originated in India before Christ Jesus, and which now can be learned in the West through numerous and varied organizations or courses. (149)

Possible Journal and/or Discussion Issues   *Phase IV*
for This Session

Whether you are working alone, in a journal, or with a group in a facilitated discussion setting, you may want to identify your own related experiences and compare them to the issues presented in this session's theme.

To help you find and clarify your own truths and extend your application of these issues, your journal comments and/or group contributions could include your thoughts about the following:

◊ In what ways have you provided times, places or routines that bring silence into your daily life? What value has this added to you (and others)?

◊ How might you increase silence periods in your day, week, month (etc.) and why—or why not—might this benefit your existence. (E.g. how would it affect health; productivity; creative life, etc.?)

◊ What might be the risks, or negative aspects, of inviting silence into your life and why (and in what ways) are you willing (or unwilling) to move ahead with this direction?

Scriptural Readings   *Phase V*
(Silent)

Psalm 23
1 The Lord is my shepherd,
  I shall not want.
2 He makes me lie down in green pastures;
  He leads me beside quiet waters.

3   He restores my soul;
He guides me in the paths of righteousness
For His name's sake.

4   Even though I walk through the valley of the shadow of death,
I fear no evil; for Thou art with me;
Thy rod and Thy staff, they comfort me.

5   Thou dost prepare a table before me in the presence of my
enemies;
Thou hast anointed my head with oil;
My cup overflows.

6   Surely goodness and lovingkindness will follow me all the days
of my life,
And I will dwell in the house of the Lord forever.

(Optional) Matthew 4, all.

Scriptural Readings
(Oral—Preappointed Reader and Discussion)

Matthew 4:1, 11; Psalm 46:4–5, 7, 10–11

Ecumenical/Inter-Faith Ideas   *Phase VI*
(Oral)

From Teton Sioux—Vision Quest of Brave Buffalo

When I was ten years old, I dreamed a dream, and in my dream
a buffalo appeared to me . . . [it] said, "Rise and follow me." I
obeyed. He took a path, and I followed. The path led upward
and was smooth like smooth black rock. It was a narrow path,
just wide enough for us to travel. We went upward a long distance and came to a tent made of buffalo hide, the door of
which faced us. . . . I found the tent filled with buffalo and was
placed in the midst of them.

The chief buffalo told me that I had been selected to represent
them in life. He said the buffalo play a larger part in life than
men realize, and in order that I might understand the buffalo

better day by day they gave me a plain stick (or cane) and told me that when I looked at it I should remember that I had been appointed to represent them. The cane was similar to the one I now carry and have carried for many years. I would not part with this cane for a fortune.[2]

◊

... You wander restlessly from forest to forest while the Reality is within your own dwelling.

The truth is here! Go where you will—to Benaves or Mathura; until you have found God in your soul, the whole world will seem meaningless to you.

Kabir (Hindu Saint)[3]

Closing Discussion and Follow-Up   *Phase VII*

Consider this session's theme in light of your own daily life, paying attention (without force and only as you are able) to the way in which you sow the seeds of confusion and restlessness into your experience. Conversely, notice how you beget calmness and order. Observe yourself carefully and with neutrality so you can discover how you yourself influence even insignificant events.

Contrast those times when you are nervous or stressed to the times you bring silence into your attitudes and behaviors. Before starting something (e.g. pouring a cup of tea; making your bed; walking to the store; feeding your children or your pets, etc.) first notice how you color the action. Do you tint your world with interior chaos, "noise" or your settled mind?

With consideration, gently that is, reflect on whatever insights arise. Watch over yourself in terms of your own pace and style. Time and such watching may reveal the obvious: that silence is enough for those who would sanctify their lives, while for others, nothing is ever enough. Practice the way of such silence (when, if and however you can). This path of pure awareness is a way without words.

◊ ◊

Appendix

ON THE CHOICE AND ROLE
OF FACILITATORS

———————— ◊ ————————

*To serve as a cook in the [Zen meditation hall] means that the
monk has attained some understanding about Zen, for it is one of
the positions highly honored in the monastery and may be filled
only by one of those who have passed a number of years here. . . .
The only desire the worker cherishes in the execution of his service
is to turn its merit to the general treasure-house of All-knowledge.*

D. T. Suzuki

As a discussion tool, *A Way Without Words* is designed to be used
by trained facilitators—individuals who understand spiritual themes,
who don't automatically link this to "dysfunction" and who know something about the subtleties and powerful potentials of group process.
Facilitation of a study group on adult spirituality seems a highly honor-
able roll. Spiritual directors, the clergy, transpersonal or Jungian analysts
can benefit a group enormously with sensitive, skilled facilitation. But
such groups bog down unproductively or drift aimlessly when trained
leadership is missing.

For example, in structuring the various phases, facilitators may want
to make a schedule at the first meeting naming readers for subsequent
sessions. This allows designated readers to prepare ahead of time. Members of the group can rotate turns, reading the opening verse, the chapter's main themes, scriptural and ecumenical readings.

A group's facilitator prepares questions and discussion points for
each session, moves things along and spots potential discussion high-
lights or problems in a way that enhances the group's learning and progress. It is beyond the scope and intent of this book to outline all the do's
and don'ts of group process. Almost every church, college or even adult-
education centers have names of local, well-trained group facilitators
who might productively use the sessions to nurture spiritual sensibilies

within a study-circle context. Even so, there may be times when com-plex, emotional or psychological problems surface. Then private coun-seling seems in order. For example, many involved in spiritual transitions (taking steps to grow whole) can find themselves revisiting certain pain-ful memories or unresolved, childhood traumas. Well-qualified, experi-enced group leaders can be gifted guides and can pinpoint these times for those individuals.

If the facilitator is a credentialed therapist or counselor, so much the better. Facilitators might also want to pre-identify qualified, certified and competent counselors in their local community before starting the first session and make sure that a list of these names is distributed to the participants along with the cautionary word that if anyone feels that old unfinished psychological business surfaces during the meetings, they consult a therapist.

If a trained facilitator is not available, a group might enlist the help of a local clergy person or educator to help them find one. Often, college or university faculty members are willing to participate in discus-sion groups as part of their course designs. Local counseling centers, synagogues or YMCAs and YWCAs are other excellent resources for finding a facilitator for your group, and such services are generally rea-sonably priced.*

If you prefer to work alone rather than with a discussion group, the exercises and scriptural passages in this book can be easily adapted to journal work. Both the oral and the silent readings are recommended, even when individuals work on their own. You may find it helpful to do your reading at the same time daily. I read for a few minutes every morn-ing even when on a business trip and find that the habit orders my mind for the whole day.

If you eventually do form, or join, a discussion group, you can bring your journal to the sessions. I do not, however, recommend that the more personal aspects of anyone's journal be made public or shared in socializing-type conversation. The primary reason for bringing a journal

---

*While it is also outside the scope of this book to discuss fees or payment issues, it is certainly worth saying that trained professionals expect to be reimbursed for their time. Often we spend vast sums for tickets to movies and rock concerts, but expect teachers, priests, ministers or psychologists to work for free.

to a group would be to refresh our memory about our insights, but this could also be accomplished by a few minutes' review of the journal at home prior to meetings.

Structure

Some structure seems necessary for almost all effective reading and especially for discussion groups. Whether this routine grows out of a common theme or is simply a way of managing the session's time seems less important than that a minimally orderly progression occur. Facilitators should try to maintain spontaneity and openness within the bounds of the suggested process while not necessarily invoking a rigid form or the ritualized (but rather deadening) feeling that "We're going through each of these steps if it kills us."

I recommend striking a healthy, easy balance between an inflexible, overly formal structure and a too-loose, unplanned or intensely emotional, "touchy-feely" environment where people are rewarded for excessively self-involved (and usually unproductive) introspection. My own tendency is to err toward the cool, somewhat cerebral side. No group or group leader is perfect; the benefits flow from the trusted, accepting relationships we establish and from our own and others' insights.

The ideal solution is if facilitators can establish an educational, study-circle setting. Here broad-gauged ideas and personal discovery are paramount. This way, both facilitators and group members can make sure that they not think of the discussion sessions as "therapy," while establishing a therapeutic process that encourages growth, support, personal development, authentic self-valuing, and so forth. As I have tried to underscore in my writings, wholesome growth is nurtured by wholesome, positive words, images and expressions, so discussion members should make every effort to discipline themselves—and their group— toward a productive, optimistic tone while not creating a Pollyannaish or artificial "Don't Worry, Be Happy" mentality. The educational model, the true dialogue or open-forum, the study-circle—all these are timeless servants.

Involvement

Discussion sessions are most lively and beneficial when each member takes some responsibility for the conversation. A contributing participant is neither passive nor dominating and controlling; the best facilitators deflect ultra-aggressiveness, draw out those who are shy or timid, and discourage those who would use the group for personal therapy.

People grow healthier and more sane when they are involved productively and repeatedly in a nurturing and intellectually honest setting with emotionally stable, non-judgmental, accepting, others. Facilitators may find it helpful to include their own personal stories and references in the discussion, but it seems detrimental to the group as a whole if leaders dominate group time and exploit the fact that they have a captive audience to expound on their own problems. The most effective facilitators continually watch themselves so that they don't use groups as a cathartic.

Preparation

Each session in this guide is correlated with the like-numbered chapter in *Ordinary People as Monks and Mystics*: Session 1 relates to Chapter 1, Session 2 to Chapter 2, and so on. Footnotes in this guide also direct readers to appropriate pages.

1. Read (or reread) the chapter relevant to the topic at hand and/or read the session overview before meeting to discuss it.

2. Pre-read *Ordinary People as Monks and Mystics*, also Thomas Merton's *Life and Holiness* (see bibliography), and perhaps any one of the several books listed in each chapter's Notes. Outside reading is, of course, optional.

3. Each participant should write out one (or more) sentences from the session's overview which he or she feels best summarizes it.

4. Read and write down one (or more) specific scriptural references to help deepen everyone's understanding of the chapter's universal themes. This will also let each individual bring his or her unique thinking process, discernment and contextual relevancies to the group. These selections (that readers bring to the group) will augment richly those provided in this book and also will broaden the discussion. My aim in listing scriptural texts and other inspirational material is to help create a context for intellectual fellowship relative to spiritual ideas.

5. Members should bring with them to each session a copy of this book, a Bible and *Ordinary People as Monks and Mystics* as well as any other scriptural texts they wish to read.

During each meeting, groups might consider tackling no more than a single theme (or chapter of *Ordinary People as Monks and Mystics*) although some groups may choose to devote more than one meeting to each chapter. It also seems practical to suggest that each discussion session last one to two hours, depending on the number of members and their involvement in that session's particular theme.

During the editing process several chapters were trimmed from the final version of this book in an attempt to keep it from being too long. It was mutually decided to delete the final three reading sessions. With hopes that this book (and its sessions) stimulates an ongoing inquiry process about adult spiritual growth, I list these sessions' themes below. Facilitators may wish to pursue these on their own, using *Ordinary People as Monks and Mystics* as a background text. Appropriate pages are indicated in parentheses.

◊ **What "form" do your illumination experiences take?**
An important exploration session in which group members may wish to understand their own peak experiences more fully. (Pages 93–95 of Chapter 7, *Ordinary People as Monks and Mystics*.)

◊ **How might you gain inner peace and self-acceptance?**
This theme addresses self-defeating attitudes and habits, and their diminishment in the face of the unitive state of God-consciousness. (Chapter 10, *Ordinary People as Monks and Mystics*.)

◊ **Are you free to choose an authentic life?**
This issue revolves around the external obstacles and inner blocks we arrange to avoid authenticity. (Pages 133–138 of Chapter 11, *Ordinary People as Monks and Mystics*.)

◊

It seems an understatement to say that groups could reunite, six months or even one year after completing a full cycle of exploration, to repeat the entire process on, hopefully, an elevated, more enlightened level of inquiry.

As both a member and a facilitator, I have directly experienced the benefits that come from working with a well-run group. When sensitive, empathic and focused leaders are at the helm, the dynamic can heal—especially when these sessions are conducted with keen respect and appreciation for the tender sensibilities of those who ultimately reveal themselves to others.

However, I've never participated in a group that combines both silence and structured reading and discussion of substantive, spiritual issues. These must exist, but I've not been in such settings. I believe this book initiates a new type of reflective process. Individuals can use this by themselves, and clerics, spiritual directors and others (like educators or those in the healing/helping professions) can easily adopt it as a vehicle by which to help group members (and themselves) grow into a greater awareness of that love which Buckminster Fuller called "omni-inclusive, progressively exquisite and compassionately attuned to other than self." Furthering a wholesome consciousness of love is my central aim in this book, since vitality in human affairs and spirituality exists to the degree to which we love or worship that which is beyond or higher than ourselves. *So comes love* (e.e. cummings).

BIBLIOGRAPHY

———— ◊ ————

Adels, J. (ed.). *The Wisdom of the Saints*. New York: Oxford University Press, 1987.

Al Chung-Laing Huang. *Embrace Tiger, Return to Mountain*. New York: Bantam Books, 1974.

Al-Ghazzali, H.M. *The Confessions of Al Ghazzali*. Trans. C. Field. Lahore: Ashraf Press (n.d.).

Anon. *Thoughts of St. Thérèse*. Rockford: Tan Books, 1915.

Aresteh, A. Reza. *Anxious Search*. Perspective Analysis Institute. Tehran: Amire Kabir Press, 1959.

———. *Rumi: The Persian, The Sufi*. London: Routledge & Kegan Paul, 1974.

Baba, Meher. *Life at Its Best*. New York: Perennial Library, Harper & Row, 1957.

Baker Eddy, Mary. *Science and Health with Key to the Scriptures*. Boston: First Church of Christ Scientist, 1971.

Bancroft, Anne. *Zen*. New York: Thames and Hudson, 1979.

Banner, Bob. "Mysticism and Psychotherapy: An Interview with Marsha Sinetar," *Critique*, Santa Rosa, California.

Bolt, Robert. *A Man for All Seasons*. New York: Scholastic Book Services, 1962 ed.

Bonhoeffer, Dietrich. *The Cost of Discipleship.* New York: Macmillan Publishing, 1937, trans.

Browning, Peter. *John Muir: In His Own Words.* LaFayette: Great West Books, 1988.

Brunton, Paul. *The Religious Urge, The Reverential Life.* Burdett: Larson Publications, 1988.

Buber, Martin (ed. Paul Medes-Slohr). *Ecstatic Confessions.* San Francisco: Harper & Row, 1985.

————. *The Way of Response.* New York: Schocken Books, 1966.

————. *Two Types of Faith.* New York: Harper Torchbooks (The Cloister Library), 1951.

Bucke, Richard. *Cosmic Consciousness.* New York: E.P. Dutton & Co., 1969.

Campbell, Joseph. *The Hero with a Thousand Faces.* Bollingen Series XVII. Princeton: Princeton University Press, 1972 ed.

Chesterton, G.K. *St. Thomas Aquinas.* New York: Doubleday/Image Books, 1956.

cummings, e.e. *100 Selected Poems.* New York: Grove Press, 1926.

Dalai Lama, in *For the Love of God* (eds. Shield and Carlson). San Raphael: New World Library, 1990.

Dass, Ram. *The Only Dance There Is.* Garden City: Anchor Books/ Doubleday, 1974.

Elgin, Duane. *Voluntary Simplicity.* New York: William Morrow and Company, 1981.

Erikson, Erik. *Insight & Responsibility.* New York: W.W. Norton, 1964.

Fromm, Erich. *The Art of Loving*. New York: Harper/Colophon, 1956.

Gandhi, M.K. *All Men Are Brothers*. New York: Continuum Publishing, 1980.

Gendler, Ruth. *Book of Qualities*. New York: Harper & Row, 1984.

Godman, David, ed. *Be As You Are: The Teachings of Sri Ramana Maharishi*. London: Arkana, 1985.

Hammarskjöld, Dag. *Markings*. New York: Alfred A. Knopf, 1976.

Henkoff, Ronald. "Is Greed Dead?" *Fortune*, August 14, 1989.

Hesse, Hermann. *Demian*. New York: Harper & Row, 1990.

Humphreys, Christmas. *The Buddhist Way of Life*. London: Mandala Books/Unwin Paperback, 1988.

Jung, Carl. *The Development of Personality*. Trans. by R.F.C. Hull. New York: Bollingen, 1954.

Karman, James. *Robinson Jeffers*. San Francisco: Chronicle Books, 1987.

Kempis, Thomas à. *Imitation of Christ*. New York: Image Books, 1955.

Kieckhefer, Richard. *Unquiet Souls*. Chicago: University of Chicago Press, 1984.

Lawson, R.P. (trans.). *Origen, The Song of Songs* (Commentary and Homilies). Ramsey: Newman Press, 1956.

Lutyens, Mary. *Krishnamurti: The Years of Fulfillment*. New York: A Discus Book/Avon Books, 1983.

Magnus, R. *Goethe as a Scientist*. Trans. Heinz Norden. New York: Henry Shuman Co., 1949.

Maslow, Abraham. *Toward a Psychology of Being.* New Jersey: D. Van Nostrand, Inc., 1962.

McDermott, Robert, ed. *The Essential Aurobindo.* New York: Schocken Books, 1973.

Merton, Thomas. *Bread in the Wilderness.* Collegeville: Liturgical Press and New Directions Publishing Company, 1986.

————. *Contemplation in a World of Action.* New York: Doubleday-Image Books, 1973.

————. *Life & Holiness.* Garden City: Image Books, 1962.

————. *The Religious Institution.* Credence Cassettes. Kansas City: National Catholic Reporter Publishing Co., 1988.

Miller, Alice. *The Drama of the Gifted Child.* New York: Basic Books, 1981.

Miller, David. *Christs.* New York: Seabury, 1981.

Monte, Christopher. *Beneath the Mask.* New York: Praeger, 1977.

New Webster's Dictionary. New York: Delair Publishing, 1981.

Newsweek, "A Time to Seek," December 17, 1990, pp. 50–56.

Peace Pilgrim, *Steps Toward Inner Peace.* Hemet: Friends of Peace Pilgrim, p. 26.

Picard, Max. *The World of Silence.* South Bend: Regnery/Gateway Inc., 1952.

Powell, James N. *The Tao of Symbols.* New York: Quill, 1982.

Roberts, Bernadette. *The Path to No-Self.* Boston: Shambhala Books, 1985.

Saint John of the Cross. *Dark Night of the Soul.* New York: Image Books, 1959.

Shields, B. and R. Carlson. *For the Love of God.* California: New World Library, 1990.

Sinetar, Marsha. *Developing a 21st Century Mind.* New York: Villard Books, 1991.

———. *Living Happily Ever After.* New York: Villard Books, 1990.

———. *Ordinary People as Monks and Mystics.* Mahwah: Paulist Press, 1986.

———. "Who Speaks?" in *For the Love of God.* San Raphael: New World Library, 1990.

Smart, Ninian and Richard D. Hecht, eds. *Sacred Texts of the World.* New York: Crossroad, 1988.

Suzuki, D.T. *Training of the Zen Buddhist Monk.* New York: Globe Press, 1934.

Swami Paramananda. *Silence as Yoga.* Cohasset: The Vedanta Centre, 1974.

Swami Prabhavananda and Christopher Isherwood, trans. *How To Know God* (The Yoga Aphorisms of Patanjali). New York: Mentor Books/New American Library, 1969.

Swami Vivekananda. *Karma Yoga and Bhakti Yoga.* New York: Rama-krishna-Vivekananda Center of New York, 1955.

Taniguchi, Masaharu. *Divine Education and Spiritual Training of Mankind.* Akasaka, Tokyo, Japan: Seicho-No-Ie Foundation, No. 5, 1956.

———. *Truth of Life* (series), Seicho-No-Ie. Gardena: 1979.

Thich Nhat Hahn. "The Peace of Divine Reality," in *For the Love of God.* San Raphael: New World Library, 1990.

Tillich, Paul. *The Courage To Be.* Binghamton: Yale University Press and Vail-Ballou Press, 1952.

Vivekananda. *Karma Yoga.* New York: Rama Krishna-Vivekananda Center, 1955.

Vlastos, Gregory, in *Choice Is Always Ours*, ed. D. Phillips. Wheaton: Re-Quest Books, 1977.

Westerman, Claus. *Handbook to the Old Testament.* Minneapolis: Augsburg Publishing House, 1976.

Wijayaratna, Mohan. *Buddhist Monastic Life.* New York: Cambridge University Press, 1990.

NOTES

———————— ◇ ————————

Introduction

1. Swami Vivekananda, *Karma Yoga*. New York: Rama Krishna-Vivekananda Center, 1955, p. 83.
2. Paul Brunton, *The Religious Urge, The Reverential Life*. New York: Larson Publications, 1988.
3. R.P. Lawson, (ed.), *Origen*, The Song of Songs. Ramsey: Newman Press, 1956.

1. Our Spiritual Intelligence

1. *New Webster's Dictionary*. New York: Delair Publishing, 1981, p. 1467.
2. Ibid.
3. Richard Bucke, *Cosmic Consciousness*. New York: E.P. Dutton & Co., 1969.
4. Marsha Sinetar, *Living Happily Ever After*. New York: Villard Books, 1990.
5. Carl Jung, *The Development of Personality*. Trans. by R.F.C. Hull. New York: Bollingen, 1954.
6. Marsha Sinetar, *Developing a 21st Century Mind*. New York: Villard Books, 1991.
7. Abraham Maslow, *Toward a Psychology of Being*. New Jersey: D. Van Nostrand Inc., 1962.
8. Erich Fromm, *The Art of Loving*. New York: Harper/Colophon, 1956.
9. Richard, Kieckhefer, *Unquiet Souls*. Chicago: University of Chicago Press, 1984.

2. From Personal Self to Universal Self

1. Dag Hammarskjöld, *Markings*. New York: Alfred A. Knopf, 1976.
2. Claus Westerman, *Handbook to the Old Testament*. Minneapolis: Augsburg Publishing House, 1976.
3. Alice Miller, *The Drama of the Gifted Child*. New York: Basic Books, 1981.
4. Marsha Sinetar, *Developing a 21st Century Mind*. New York: Villard Books, 1991.
5. Erik Erikson, *Insight & Responsibility*. New York: W.W. Norton, 1964.
6. Marsha Sinetar, *Ordinary People as Monks and Mystics*. Mahwah: Paulist Press, 1986.
7. Marsha Sinetar, *Developing a 21st Century Mind*. New York: Villard Books, 1991.
8. M.K. Gandhi, *All Men Are Brothers*. New York: Continuum Publishing, 1980, p. 105.
9. Ronald Henkoff, "Is Greed Dead?" *Fortune*, August 14, 1989, p. 40.

3. Resisting Our Good

1. Duane Elgin, *Voluntary Simplicity*. New York: William Morrow and Company, 1981.
2. Marsha Sinetar, *Ordinary People as Monks and Mystics*. Mahwah: Paulist Press, 1986.
3. Christopher Monte, *Beneath the Mask*. New York: Praeger, 1977, p. 58.
4. Paul Tillich, *The Courage To Be*. New Haven: Yale University Press, and Binghamton: Vail-Ballou Press, 1952.
5. Mary Lutyens, *Krishnamurti: The Years of Fulfillment*. New York: A Discus Book/Avon Books, 1983.
6. Marsha Sinetar, *Developing a 21st Century Mind*. New York: Villard Books, 1991.
7. Acts 17:11.
8. Eph 5:15.
9. Christopher Monte, *Beneath the Mask*. New York: Praeger, 1977, p. 470.

10. Heb 12:12.
11. Ibid.
12. Ibid.
13. 2 Cor 8:11.
14. Anon., *Thoughts of St. Thérèse*. Rockford: Tan Books, 1915, p. 45.
15. Anne Bancroft, *Zen*. New York: Thames and Hudson, 1979, p.29.

4. Identification for Rebirth

1. Erich Fromm, *The Art of Loving*. New York: Harper/Colophon, 1956, p. 112.
2. Ruth Gendler, *Book of Qualities*. New York: Harper & Row, 1984, p. 69.
3. Swami Vivekananda, *Karma Yoga*. New York: Rama Krishna-Vivekananda Center, 1955.
4. A. Reza Aresteh, *Rumi (The Persian, The Sufi)*. London: Routledge & Kegan Paul, 1965, p. 277.
5. David Miller, *Christs*. New York: Seabury, 1981.
6. Al Chung-Laing Huang, *Embrace Tiger, Return to Mountain*. New York: Bantam Books, 1974.
7. Marsha Sinetar, *Ordinary People as Monks and Mystics*. Mahwah: Paulist Press, 1986.
8. Bob Banner, "Mysticism and Psychotherapy: Interview," *Critique Magazine*, Santa Rosa, California.
9. Joseph Campbell, *The Hero with a Thousand Faces*. Bollingen Series XVII. Princeton: Princeton University Press, 1972 ed.

5. The Solitary Revolution

1. Alice Miller, *The Drama of the Gifted Child*. New York: Basic Books, 1981, pp. 83, 85.
2. Hermann Hesse, *Demian*. New York: Harper & Row, 1990, p. 127.
3. Mt 4:7.

6. Nothing Special

1. Marsha Sinetar, *Ordinary People as Monks and Mystics*. Mahwah: Paulist Press, 1986.
2. Mt 13:45–46.

3. Gregory Vlastos in *Choice Is Always Ours,* ed. D. Phillips. Wheaton: Re-Quest Books, 1977.

4. G.K. Chesterton, *St. Thomas Aquinas.* New York: Doubleday/Image Books, 1956.

5. Mt 9:17.

6. Bernadette Roberts, *The Path to No-Self.* Boston: Shambhala Books, 1985.

7. Eph 6:7.

8. Ram Dass, *The Only Dance There Is.* New York: Doubleday, 1974.

9. Paul Brunton, *The Religious Urge, the Reverential Life.* Burdett: Larson Publications, 1988, p. 74.

10. Sri Aurobindo (ed: Robert McDermott), *The Essential Aurobindo.* New York: Schocken Books, 1973.

11. Ibid., p. 162.

12. Ibid.

13. Christmas Humphreys, *The Buddhist Way of Life.* London: Mandala Books/Unwin Paperback, 1988, p. 136.

7. Impersonal Love's Ordinariness

1. Thomas Merton, *Life & Wholeness.* Garden City: Image Books, 1962, p. 29.

2. Ibid.

3. Max Picard, *The World of Silence.* South Bend: Regency/Gateway, Inc., 1952.

4. Martin Buber, *Ecstatic Confessions.* (ed. Paul Mendes Flohr). San Francisco: Harper & Row, 1985, p. 77.

5. A. Reza Aresteh, *Rumi (The Persian, The Sufi).* London: Routledge & Kegan Paul, 1965, p. 76.

8. Our Bread of Heaven

1. Thomas Merton, *The Religious Institution.* Credence Cassettes. Kansas City: National Catholic Reporter Publishing Co., 1988.

2. 1 Tim 2:6-7.

3. Thomas Merton, *The Religious Institution.* Credence Cassettes. Kansas City: National Catholic Reporter Publishing Co., 1988.

4. R.P. Lawson, (trans.), *Origen,* The Song of Songs (Commentary & Homilies). Ramsey: Newman Press, 1956, pp. 9–10.

5. Peter Browning, *John Muir: In His Own Words.* LaFayette: Great West Books, 1988.
6. Martin Buber, *Two Types of Faith.* New York: Harper Torchbooks (The Cloister Library), 1951.
7. Thomas Merton, *Bread in the Wilderness.* Collegeville: Liturgical Press and New Directions Publishing Company, 1986.
8. Ibid.
9. The Dalai Lama in *For the Love of God* (eds. Shield and Carlson). San Raphael: New World Library, 1990, p. 3.
10. Thomas Merton, *Bread in the Wilderness.* Collegeville: Liturgical Press and New Directions Publishing Company, 1986.
11. Thich Nhat Hahn. "The Peace of Divine Reality," in *For the Love of God.* San Raphael: New World Library, 1990, p. 127.
12. Marsha Sinetar, "Who Speaks?" in *For the Love of God.* San Raphael: New World Library, 1990.
13. Rom 10:10.
14. Robert Bolt, *A Man for All Seasons,* p. ix.
15. Mohan Wijayaratna, *Buddhist Monastic Life.* New York: Cambridge University Press, 1990, p. 89.
16. A. Reza Aresteh, *Rumi: The Persian, The Sufi.* London: Routledge & Kegan Paul, 1974.
17. James N. Powell, *The Tao of Symbols.* New York: Quill, 1982, p. 233.

Session 1

1. H.M. Al-Ghazzali, *The Confessions of Al Ghazzali* (translated by C. Field). Lahore: Ashraf Press (n.d.), pp. 50–51.
2. Ninian Smart and Richard D. Hecht, eds., *Sacred Texts of the World.* New York: Crossroad, 1988, p. 42.
3. Christmas Humphreys, *The Buddhist Way of Life.* London: Mandala Books/Unwin Paperback, 1988, p. 33.

Session 2

1. Paul Brunton, *The Religious Urge; The Reverential Life.* New York: Larson Publications, 1988, p. 24.
2. Ninian Smart and Richard D. Hecht, eds., *Sacred Texts of the World.* New York: Crossroad, 1988, p. 348.

3. Swami Prabhavananda and Christopher Isherwood, trans., *How To Know God* (The Yoga Aphorisms of Patanjali). Mentor Books/New American Library: The Vedanta Society of Southern California, 1953, p. 36.

Session 3

1. e.e. cummings, *100 Selected Poems*. New York: Grove Press, 1926, p. 18.
2. Swami Vivekananda, *Karma Yoga and Bhakti Yoga*. New York: Ramakrishna-Vivekananda Center of New York, 1955, p. 10.
3. Ninian Smart and Richard D. Hecht, eds., *Sacred Texts of the World*. New York: Crossroad, 1988, p. 193.

Session 4

1. Peace Pilgrim, *Steps Toward Inner Peace*. Friends of Peace Pilgrim, Hemet, California 92344, p. 26. (Phone 714-927-7678 for a copy of her inspiring booklet.)
2. Dr. Masaharu Taniguchi, *Divine Education and Spiritual Training of Mankind*. Akasaka, Tokyo, Japan: Seicho-No-Ie Foundation, 1956, No. 5, pp. 134-5.
3. Ninian Smart and Richard D. Hecht, eds., *Sacred Texts of the World*. New York: Crossroad, 1988, p. 284.

Session 5

1. Martin Buber, *The Way of Response*. New York: Schocken Books, 1966, p. 136.
2. Ninian Smart and Richard D. Hecht, eds., *Sacred Texts of the World*. New York: Crossroad, 1988, p. 367.

Session 6

1. Mary Lutyens, *Krishnamurti: The Years of Fulfillment*. New York: A Discus Book/Avon Books, 1983, p. 164.
2. Mk 2:17.
3. Ninian Smart and Richard D. Hecht, eds., *Sacred Texts of the World*. New York: Crossroad, 1988, p. 315.
4. Ibid., p. 336.

Session 7

1. Max Picard, *The World of Silence*. South Bend: Regnery/Gateway Inc., 1952.
2. Ninian Smart and Richard D. Hecht, eds., *Sacred Texts of the World*. New York: Crossroad, 1988, p. 359.
3. Swami Prabhavananda and Christopher Isherwood. *How To Know God*. New York: Mentor Books, New American Library, 1969, p. 53.

About the Author

Marsha Sinetar is a leading exponent of the practical value of self-actualization. Long immersed in the study of creatively-gifted, spiritually-emerging adults, her findings are published in several books increasingly used worldwide in colleges and universities, by therapists and spiritual directors, and by spiritual seekers from diverse traditions. Dr. Sinetar began her career as a teacher and moved rapidly through the ranks of public education as a principal, curriculum specialist and university lecturer. In 1980, after earning a Ph.D. in psychology, she founded her own corporate psychology firm (Santa Rosa, California) and for years has advised top management of Fortune 500 corporations on issues of leadership and rapid organizational change. Marsha Sinetar presently lives "as quietly as possible" at her home among the coastal redwoods of the Pacific northwest. Persons wishing more information about workshops and support programs for helping professionals may send a business-sized self-addressed envelope to Dr. Marsha Sinetar, PO Box 1, Stewarts Point, CA 95480.